CW00417820

THE GREAT DEHYDRATOR COOKBOOK

Preserve vegetables, fruits, meats, herbs and more, making jerky, fruit leather & just-add-water meals

Philip Kuckunniw

—

Copyright

Philip Kuckunniw

Disclaimer

Table of Contents

Introduction

Welcome to the wonderful world of dehydration. Not only is it a way to store food for later enjoyment, but it will make you think of a new way of cooking! You will find yourself using things like dried cherries, papaya and even seafood. Dehydrated foods can be stored for a long time, saving money and shelf space and can add exciting new flavours to your dishes.

Once you start storing food this way, it's hard to stop doing it because you see so many possibilities. Before you know it, it's a new hobby. You will also find that you can use a dehydrator for things other than drying food.

You can make your own yogurt or use the dehydrator to let the homemade bread rise. How cool is it? You can make homemade granola and energy bars at a fraction of the cost of those purchased in the store, you will also know what it contains. And if you have a limited budget, you can dry the remaining foods to keep them for a long time. The possibilities are endless!

PART I

In this section you will find everything you need to know about dehydrating food. Even if you've never dried anything before or never used a dehydrator, don't worry because when you get to the end of this part, you'll be an expert.

WHAT IS DEHYDRATION?

Not only have humans hunted and collected food since the beginning of time; we have also preserved it. There is nothing new in extending the shelf life of the food we grow or buy. By drying the food we make sure that there is always something available in the closet that is good and nutritious to eat. If you've never thought about drying food before, once you find out how much fun it is, you may not be able to re-milk or freeze the food again.

There is a good chance that one of your ancestors will dry things like fruits and vegetables. In fact, it is the oldest method of storing food.

Early civilizations used the sun and wind to dry berries, roots and even herbs. Native American tribes and early American settlers dried food to survive both the drought and the harsh winters.

Dehydration may seem complicated, but the process is simple.

Food has high water content. When food is dried, most of this water is removed, which prevents the growth of organisms such as yeasts, enzymes and bacteria, which all lead to deterioration. Fruits and vegetables are made up of about 80-95 percent water and meats are made up of 50-75 percent water. Dehydration reduces the water content to about 10 percent, leaving most of the complete nutritional value of food intact. Dehydration also acts as a natural food preservative.

But, could you say, how about boxing? What about freezing? What's wrong with these conservation methods? Here are some reasons why many people choose to dry over other food storage methods.

Less time and skill are required. If you've ever tried to box and give up because things didn't go according to plan, comfort: dehydrating food is much simpler and less time consuming. Even if you've never done it before, dehydrating is a skill that you can quickly learn and actually become an expert. And let's be honest: who really wants to spend time storing food in mid-summer when their kitchen already looks 110 ° F. The use of a dehydrating machine produces very little heat, so you will not lose your temper even if you are at 90 ° F outside and you run the machine all day.

Less storage space is needed. The era of life in large houses is over and today many of us have moved to smaller houses.
Maybe your adult children have moved in or your family has had a recent new addition. Either way, we need to make the most of the space we have. The last thing we want to do is fill the shelves with canned food or even a horizontal

freezer that occupies precious feet in the basement or garage. Dehydration reduces food to one tenth of its original size, so one pound of carrots can easily fit into a small jar.

If you have a small kitchen or limited storage space, dehydration is for you.

Capture the flavor when it is fresh. One of the best things about summer is the abundance and variety of products. However, a big disadvantage is when it's hot and the food spoils quickly and you can only eat a lot. Dehydration allows you to have the best of both worlds.

It is worth preserving. We all love to eat something tasty and sweet between meals. When you dehydrate the fruits, their flavors not only become more concentrated, but they also become sweeter and are therefore the ideal snack for children and adults.

Get maximum nutrition. You have heard it over and over; turn on the television and there is a nutritionist who tells us to eat five portions of fruit and vegetables a day. We know it makes sense, but sometimes it's not easy to compress them. You can solve the problem with some dried fruit for breakfast cereals or in that brown sack lunch. Dried foods as soon as you take them home with all the essential flavours, colours and nutrients. Many people think it's as good as eating fresh food.

Enjoy foods without preservatives. If you are a label detective, you will know that even a bag of apricots can contain ingredients that justify the decoding of an advanced level in chemistry. Dry your food and you will always know what's inside.

Save Money. Taking care of your food budget? With the continuous increase in prices in the supermarket, who does not care about inflation and how to feed their family? You will be great to earn money when you become an avid dehydrator. When the food is abundant, it is at its lowest price and you can make a deal. It is a good time to store and store all types of food for later use when prices rise.

Save on storage and equipment. Using an electric dehydrator will cost you half the preserves and almost seven times less than freezing. And just think about the money you will save because you no longer need jars and a supply of new lids every year.

Preserve your garden. Maybe you're one of the many people who like to grow vegetables in their backyard. Now you have no reason to throw away that pile of zucchini or a tub of tomatoes. Drying them is an easy and inexpensive way to store them for future meals. And it's not just an excess of fresh produce that you can dry. If you open a can of tomato paste and you only need a spoon, put the remaining amount in the dehydrator and keep it for another recipe.

Create emergency food supplies. Head to the Weather Channel and you will probably feel that we are going in a record season for one or the other. If you live in a hurricane or tornado-prone area, you know how important it is to have a food supply in case a storm affects your energy or water supply. Dry food is light, space efficient and easy to carry in case the worst case scenario occurs and you are forced to run away from home.

Stock up on camping gear. One of the joys of sitting around a campfire is eating food that you have brought with you. However, who wants to be weighed along a path with bean cans and soup? Dehydration makes light food and takeaway food more practical than it can fit any backpack.
We hope that now we have convinced you of how excellent dehydration is, so let's move on to some of the tools of the trade. There is more good news there because, unlike boxing, you will need fewer tools.

Dehydration of food, known as drying of food in some environments, is a method of preserving food by removing water.
Food dehydration is one of the oldest methods of drying food. It has been in use long before the invention of refrigeration systems designed to keep fresh food fresh. It is an easy to use method and one of the safest food storage methods known to man.

When done properly, dehydration allows you to store food for long periods of time without worrying about spoiling it.

Removing water from food creates an environment hostile to the growth of microorganisms and bacteria. Bacteria and mold need water to thrive. The elimination of this water creates an environment in which microorganisms cannot survive, much less grow in large colonies capable of causing chaos on stored food.

There are several methods for drying food, the most popular are:

- Sun Drying.
- Oven Drying.
- Using a commercial food dehydrator.
- Freeze Drying.

All four methods will be discussed in more detail in later chapters.

There are many foods that you can dry.

Whatever, someone has probably found a way to remove the water. These are just some of the foods that people dehydrate and store:

- Meat.
- Seafood.
- Fruit.
- Vegetables.
- Wheat.
- Herbs.

Food generally takes on a new consistency and a slightly different flavor once it has dried. They tend to shrink, darken a bit and the skin wrinkles and becomes harder. They are usually sweeter because the sugars in the foods are still there in the smaller dry foods.

You are probably already familiar with some dry foods. Finely chopped meat is transformed into dried meat. Grapes become raisins when dried. You have probably also tried other dried fruits. Apricots, bananas, papaya. . . The list goes on and on. There is an almost unlimited amount of food that can be dried.

Drying food instead of storing it or freezing it as a storage medium gives you more options when it comes to storing. Once dry, food can be stored at room temperature for a long time before you have to worry about spoiling it. Dry food is reduced to a fraction of its size before dehydration, so you don't need as much space to store dehydrated food as food stored by the other two methods.

Drying will not completely replace canning or freezing because it changes the taste and appearance of food, but it is a good change of pace.

If you are looking to spice up your meals, try adding one or two dry foods.

Hikers, backpackers and those looking to quickly escape to the forest (yes, survivors, I'm talking about you), it could be much worse than dry food. They are light and nutrient-rich, making them a good choice on the road or on the highway for drivers who want to travel light.

Most people don't understand how simple dehydrating food is.

Buying already dried food will cost you a small fortune compared to how much it costs to do it yourself. Find out how to dry food and save a penny. You will also be able to avoid many of the additives and chemicals that manufacturers add to foods when they are dried.

After preparing food, modern dryers do all the work for you.

They dry the air and circulate it through food, where the air absorbs moisture. All you need is a little common sense and the ability to follow simple instructions.

It's smart to store food! The importance of a careful family food storage program has been recognized for centuries. Until the invention of modern appliances and services, proper food storage was essential for survival. With the development of modern technology and transportation, many people have realized that it is no longer necessary to store food. However, there is value in food storage and a food storage program will benefit the average family in many ways:

1. Planning ahead to preserve seasonal food means it can be enjoyed all year round.

2. In times of crisis, proper food storage provides a life-saving source of nourishment and offers an excellent sense of security.

3. A food storage program provides a method to help reduce the cost of food. If food is purchased when it is more abundant, the price is lower.

4. Dry foods can provide delicious supplements to the fresh foods available, although often limited.

5. The remaining foods can be dehydrated to avoid food waste. For example, fruits that are too ripe to be dehydrated or dehydrated can be used in the skin of the fruit. Any part can be used; Celery tops can be dehydrated, for example, and used in soups or stewed recipes.

There are several types of food storage available for the average family. Everyone has a place and should be used to meet the family's nutritional needs. Following are the methods that you can use:

1. Dehydration or Drying
2. Canning
3. Freezing
4. Salting or Brining
5. Root Cellars
6. Jams and Jellies
7. Smoking
8. Sprouting of Stored Seeds

The Benefits of Dehydration: Dehydration has a number of benefits. Here is a list of the benefits that come to mind:

- Safe storage of food.
- All natural. No chemicals or preservatives are needed.
- You can create a food supply that you can use in an emergency when you don't have supplies.
- It allows you to bring healthy food on the go.

The biggest advantage of drying food is that it saves you money, a lot of money if you play your cards right.
That's how:

Seasonal foods are cheaper at the height of the season.
Fruits, cereals and vegetables are cheaper when harvested locally. Fish and shellfish are seasonal and cost less during the catch season. Watch out for supermarket specials during big holidays for cheap meat.
Typically, when you get a good amount of food, you can only buy what the family can consume before it goes bad. When a good business arrives, you can take advantage of it only in small quantities.

Learning to dehydrate foods allows you to buy large quantities of your favorite foods when prices are at a minimum.

Buy everything you have room to store, dry it and enjoy it long after the prices go up to inaccessible levels. Instead of living with rice and beans, you can enjoy all your favorites throughout the year.

Another way to save money is to grow your own food.

If you have space in your courtyard, you can grow a garden with your favorite fruit and vegetables. A garden is an inexpensive way to grow some of your food. It's amazing how much food you can get even from a small plot. Planting a tree or two is a good way to grow your fruit.

Even if you don't have space on your patio for a garden, you can still take advantage of the local harvest.

Farmers markets and flea markets with product sections are good places to find the best deals. You can also try contacting local farms to see if they are willing to sell directly to the public. You will probably get more mileage from small family owned farms. Visit the local docks for the best fish deals when it is in season locally.

Another way to save money is to meet a group of friends, family or like-minded people to buy bulk food.

Large quantities of food can be purchased from cooperatives at low prices. When it comes to meat, you can buy an entire slab and get it at a discount. Reach an agreement in advance about who gets what and everyone will end up getting a lot.

Those with little ownership can raise their own livestock.

Even if you don't have the stomach to cut it yourself, you can send it for a nominal fee. It is still much cheaper than buying meat at the store.

Hunters often have more meat than they know what to do. Most animal meats can be dried in delicious jerky. If you know a hunter (or are a hunter), you have an inexpensive source of meat that can be dried.

All forms of food storage work by slowing down or stopping the processes that cause food to decompose, decompose or rot. Wine preserves juice by replacing sugar with alcohol. Pickled pickles store cucumbers by converting sugar into lactic acid.

The freezing of food preserves it by slowing down the enzymatic processes and making it too cold for reproduction by decaying organisms.

Canning preserves food by killing decaying organisms, deactivating enzymes and excluding oxygen. Dehydration works by removing the water needed to make enzymes work and ruining organisms for life.

Why Foods Rot

Everything that is produced in nature returns to nature. The sheets that fall from the trees eventually become the soil from which the trees draw nourishment to create new sheets. Although food sometimes takes a more winding road to its final destination, this is the destination of all things. Nature guarantees this result in the same mechanisms as cells.

When a cell is cut out of its food and oxygen stores, as in the case of steak cells when a steering is killed, the enzymatic processes in the cell simply don't stop. In fact, these processes can continue for many days depending on the conditions in which they are stored. However, the processes are not what normally occur while the animal is alive. During life, metabolic wastes such as lactic acid and carbon dioxide are removed and replaced with fresh glucose and oxygen. This allows the cell to function effectively. But when waste is no longer disposed of and new supplies are no longer delivered, proteins and enzymes within the cell take on a different character and purpose. In particular, proteins are created that destroy hard tissues and collagen so that meat can be more easily digested by microorganisms such as bacteria and macroorganisms such as fly larvae.

While the meat aging process is sometimes considered a form of putrefaction, it isn't actually rotting because it doesn't use decaying organisms. Rather, aging occurs at temperatures that discourage rapid bacterial growth and at the same time allow the post-life enzymatic processes of the cells to soften the meat to make it tastier. Obviously, if the temperatures were a little too high or were not frozen too long, tender meat would be an excellent meal for microorganisms that would induce putrefaction in a short time.

The same goes for fruit and vegetables. For example, during pickling in brine, the end of the cucumber is cut into slices so that the enzymes do not spread through the cucumber and soften it.

So the first cause of food spoilage is enzymatic. The enzymes inside the cells of a food product break it down, soften it and prepare it for the consumption of microorganisms such as fungi and macro-organisms such as fly larvae. These enzymes do not spoil food, but rather make it susceptible to the degradation of organisms and alter its character.

Another cause of food spoilage is microorganisms. With the exception of pathogenic diseases, which occur while something is alive and livelihoods are exchanged, microorganisms rarely have much effect. An apple on a tree is rarely spoiled, the spinach sheets on a plant are not spoiled and the chickens that walk in the yard are unaffected by bacteria. Only after plant or animal cells no longer receive new livelihoods and their waste is no longer disposed of, do they become vulnerable to deterioration.

Of course, we usually don't eat apples directly from the tree or take a chicken from the yard and eat it whole in the feathered place. Instead, they are processed and shipped or collected and stored. And it is the time after collection or processing that creates the window of vulnerability for microorganisms.

Microorganisms that are completely harmless to living beings deal quickly with processed and collected food. As they consume food, their populations grow and return nutrients from food to the soil to repeat the cycle. When this happens in the compost pile, it's a good thing. When it happens on the kitchen counter with organic peaches that cost $ 5 / lb, the event is less fun.

Microorganisms are no different from any other living thing in that they require certain conditions to thrive. Some microorganisms require oxygen and others cannot grow while oxygen is present. Some microorganisms grow best at room temperature and others grow better at slightly higher or lower temperatures. Each microorganism also has certain preferred ranges of foods. This means that they will grow with some foods, but not with others.

These two factors (cellular enzymes and microorganisms) are the key factors in food spoilage. Other factors may contribute to these processes and may also be prerequisites, but enzymes and microorganisms are the key.

Sunlight and other bright light sources also play a role in deterioration because ultraviolet rays can discolor or damage food. Another source of damage is oxidation. You saw it with a cut potato or an apple that changes color. Although the changes brought about by sunlight and oxidation are not as severe as those produced by enzymes and microorganisms, preventing them is important for creating an attractive product.

How dehydration prevents food from spoiling Water is necessary for life and all vital processes. There is no life without water. While this can only be a problem if you have decided to cross the Sahara desert, it is also useful knowledge for storing food.

Water is the vector within cells that allows enzymes to function. If the water is removed from the cell, the enzymes stop on their way. Most enzymes have a particular temperature range in which they work. Freezing preserves food by keeping enzymes below their operating temperature range. Tanning preserves food by raising the temperature so high that the enzymes are denatured so that they break down and therefore cannot do anything. Dehydration works by removing the water whose enzymes are supposed to work. It is important to understand that enzymes may be (and often are) still present in dehydrated foods, but they are simply inactive due to lack of water. Once the water is added, the enzymatic action returns and the consequent degradation.

Freezing controls microbes by keeping temperatures too cold for reproduction. Boxing controls microbes by killing them at high temperatures. Dehydration controls microbes making the environment unattractive to them.

Microbes need water to live and multiply. There are some microbes that form spores and lethargy while conditions are too dry, but many microbes become dehydrated and die.

An item should not be dehydrated until it has absolutely zero humidity to store. For example, if I diluted some honey with water in a 50/50 ratio, the container containing undiluted honey would not spoil, but diluted honey would. Although undiluted honey clearly contains some water, it does not contain enough water to support bacterial growth, although diluted honey will support bacteria like crazy. Dehydration therefore disrupts the enzymatic processes and deprives the microbes of the water they need to live, thus preventing deterioration.

Which Foods can be Dehydrated?

Any vegetable, fruit, meat or bread can be dehydrated. The question is not so much whether it can be dehydrated as it makes sense, or how dehydrated food will be used.
Dehydration causes serious damage to the structural integrity of the walls of food cells. Consequently, when the dehydrated food is reconstituted by adding water, its consistency is not the same as that of the fresh product. Canned and frozen foods are very similar to fresh products, while in most cases dehydrated foods will be compact or soft. You can dehydrate beef and carrots, but dehydrated products will go much better in a soup or stew than on a main meat dish.

There are also some practical considerations. To effectively dehydrate, some foods (such as cauliflower) will have to break down the cell walls by bleaching them. Other foods such as apples can be dehydrated simply by cutting them, dipping them in a little lemon juice and putting them in the dehydrator. However, other foods are almost completely water, such as watermelon. Watermelon contains so much water that dehydration would take a long time and all that would remain would be a vague pink spot.
So while in theory practically any food can dehydrate, in practice you will want to reserve dehydration for foods whose value will improve with the process. Apples, pears and dried bananas, for example, make excellent snacks; and if you've ever looked at the prices of prepackaged dehydrators, you'll know that making your dried fruit is clearly worth the money. A hard flank steak cut into strips and dried will be very tender in a stew. Dried onion is a universal spice. Drying your homemade bread before it spoils so you can create your own filling mix will save you money during Thanksgiving and offer you a superior dining experience than mixes.

It's not just about dollars and cents, of course. Dehydrated foods can also add an element of convenience. I make lots of soups and stews over the winter, and it's nice to be able to reach out and grab a handful of dried carrots, dried celery, dried salsify or even dried red peppers to add to them.

When I prepare my spaghetti sauces instead of using a commercial thickener, after boiling it to get the right consistency, I spray some of my dried tomatoes in the blender. Absorbs excess moisture from the sauce providing an authentic tomato flavor. Drying also concentrates flavors in food, which is why much less dried basil is used in a sauce than fresh basil.

Therefore, you should dry the food that will be useful to you in a dry form. Sometimes the range of what would be useful isn't intuitively obvious. You can get some ideas by reading the ingredients in salad dressings and soup mixes. Although the first ingredient is usually salt, MSG or some type of starch, from that moment on you will always find onion, garlic, red peppers, peas and similar old friends. Once you see how dehydrated foods are used, it will quickly become clear that you can make dehydrated products that are superior to what you can buy.

Steps for Dehydration

Food dehydration involves four steps: preparation, pre-treatment, dehydration and conservation. The four steps are important for a properly stored product and the details may vary slightly depending on the specific food.

The preparation involves cleaning or washing, removing seeds or defective points, then cutting the food into slices or strips of uniform thickness between ⅛ "and ¼".

Pretreatment methods generally focus on preventing oxidation and breaking cell walls, if necessary. In the case of meat, it is also necessary to disinfect the surface by immersing it in a boiling solution.

Although dehydration can be practiced theoretically by hanging food on shelves in the sun, as is still done in some cultures, a dehydrator is needed for modern times. You can buy dehydrators in box stores or online, or you can build your own. The key features you want in a dehydrator are a fan and temperature control. Once a food is dehydrated, it will have less humidity than the ambient air and will tend to replenish the lost moisture by removing it from the air. To avoid this, dehydrated foods should be stored in airtight containers. In most cases, I use square-sized cans with closing lids, even if I sometimes use vacuum-sealed bags or airtight plastic containers. These are stored in a dark and cool place to avoid damage caused by sunlight.

Preparation

Few foods are improved in quality with any preservation method. Indeed, to some extent, the quality of a non-fresh food will always suffer. Therefore, you want to start with the best food available. If something is too mature, it's okay, and it's good to cut the rotten spots as long as you remove them completely. But you don't even want to start with foods that are clearly out of date. Flabby carrots and wilted celery will not be the best dehydrated vegetables.

The food you start with should be washed to reduce bacteria. Just pour it under the water in the sink and dry it with a paper towel. Over the past decade or so, many people have suffered from food poisoning due to commercial farmers who have carelessly applied raw manure to crops that are too close to harvest times. The crops were contaminated with E. coli or other microbes. Furthermore, it is almost impossible to guarantee that no faecal matter has come into contact with raw meat. So wash and dry it before you start. If you are processing leafy vegetables, you can dry them properly with salad roulette. I chose one for $ 10 and love it.

Foods that dehydrate must be cut into slices for proper dehydration. In general, anything from ⅛ "to ¼" is sufficient, but it is important that all the slices in a batch have more or less the same thickness. Otherwise, you will end up with some pieces that dry much earlier than others.
Cutting is also difficult to make by hand, but there are a number of inexpensive cutting guides on the market that will provide you with perfectly uniform cuts in no time. I took mine in a large pharmacy chain for $ 20. It comes with plates of varying thicknesses and lasts for years. They work very well with fruits and vegetables, but not with meat. In the chapter on building your dehydrator, I'll show you how you can create your meat cutting guide.

Pretreatment

Pretreating soft fruit and vegetables is little more than immersing the slices in a solution based on lemon juice or vitamin C mixed with water. Use 500 mg of vitamin C or two tablespoons of lemon juice for every liter of water. These acts as antioxidants to prevent drastic changes in color from exposure to oxygen as food dries. Food is perfectly safe if not pre-treated with an antioxidant, but it looks more appetizing if it is.

For fruits that are cut in half and take a long time (more than a day) to dehydrate, they are usually pretreated with a solution of potassium metabisulphite (the same material used to make wine) or sulphated by putting the fruits in a basket, closed on a burning sulfur mound. This is commonly used with apricots, peaches and nectarines. The sulfur dioxide vapors generated by sulfur combustion combine with water to form an acid that quickly forms sulphites inside the fruit. Since I do most of my dehydration in the fall and winter when the house is closed and the smell of sulfur is unpleasant, I use potassium metabisulfite in the form of Campden tablets available from home beer suppliers.

Crush a Campden tablet into one liter of water along with a vitamin C tablet.

When it comes to vegetables with a harder cell structure, their pretreatment consists of steam bleaching. Examples of vegetables that would need to be blanched include potatoes, sweet potatoes, carrots, turnips, parsnips, broccoli, cabbage and sausages. To steam the vegetables after they have been cleaned and sliced, boil them for 3-4 minutes, then immediately put them back in ice water for another 3-4 minutes. After this, dry them and then put them in your dehydrator. Turnips and potatoes would benefit from a dip in lemon juice after bleaching to avoid discoloration.

The pretreatment of unground meat is obtained by bleaching it in boiling water for a few seconds until the surface of the meat becomes gray. This is enough to kill surface bacteria. Subsequently, it is not necessary to freeze the meat, just place it in the dehydrator.

To dehydrate you need a dehydrator. Ideally, you want a model with fan and temperature control. Round models that you can buy in department stores, such as Nesco® / American Harvest®, generally provide only one square meter of shelf space and generally include only five shelves. These are fine for occasional use of small batches, but if you try to use them to store half a bushel of potatoes or even a lot of apples, you will quickly find them insufficient for the task. Dehydrators of this type are easy to clean and work great, and you can find them for as little as $ 35. So if you have enough room to run three at the same time, you can do it.

The next level of dehydrator is something like Excalibur® with fifteen square feet of space, but it has a rather high price of $ 270. If it's not practical and it's little space, it's still a good option if you expect to dehydrate yourself a lot.

A third option is to create yours. In the final chapter of this book, I describe an excellent homemade dehydrator. Depending on how tall the shelves are, you could have 32 square feet of drying space in a dehydrator which costs around $ 230 to build.

That's a lot of dehydrating money, so if you're good at hand tools and isn't intimidated by a small basic electrical wiring, building your own is the way to go. The items to be dehydrated are placed in a single layer on the shelves without overlapping, the temperature control is adjusted and the unit is turned on. Although many dehydrators are equipped with books that indicate a certain time to dehydrate various articles, these times are, at best, general hypotheses. This is because the drying time will vary with the ambient humidity, the thickness of the food, the amount of moisture in the food and the uniformity of the slices. To check if the food is cooked, remove a piece from the dehydrator and allow it to cool. Vegetables are made when they are hard or crunchy. The fruits should be flexible and leathery, but they will feel dry and will not show moisture if torn and pinched. Dried meats and fish should be hard, but flexible rather than fragile. A little oil in meat and fish is fine.

Temperature regulation is simple. Use a temperature between 90 and 100 degrees for herbs, spices and flowers to protect their flavors. Nuts and seeds should also dry from 90 to 100 degrees to prevent their delicate oils from becoming rancid. Fruits and vegetables should be dried at 130-140 degrees to protect their vitamin C content, and meats should be dried at 150-160 degrees to avoid deterioration during drying.

Storing

It is inevitable that some of the food in the dehydrator will run out sooner than the others. When the food is ready, remove it from the dehydrator and store it in an airtight container. Do not mix different foods in the same container because the flavors will have an impact. Store the containers in a cool place away from light and keep them sealed when not in use so that they do not absorb moisture from the atmosphere. The food will be stored in this way for up to one year without any problems.

If you want to store food for a long time, instead of using an airtight container, use one of the many vacuum sealers available, such as Seal-a-Meal® or FoodSaver®. Stored in this way, even at room temperature, dehydrated foods can be kept for 4-5 years. If you want to keep them even longer, put the vacuum packs on the bottom of a freezer in the chest where they will be kept for about fifteen years.

Keys to Successful Dehydration

Dehydrating requires patience. Dehydration is a slow process, but it is easy, fun and useful. Here are some general tips for success.

Humidity and Humidity

Humidity varies widely across the country, from my humid hometown of Seattle to the arid mountains of New Mexico and the humid Atlantic coast. Fruit and vegetables also vary greatly in their moisture content; You could have a juicy or starchy apple and a winter plum tomato from Mexico will be considerably less moist than the memorabilia from your summer garden. If you are drying a large number of plums, your dehydrator will fill up with moisture, so a machine full of plums will take longer to dry than a single tray.

Take your Time

Dehydrators vary widely from model to model in their operating characteristics. Standard round dehydrators are very affordable in terms of size, price and availability, but work slower than larger closed metal units with larger fans. When you have a habit of drying yourself, you will adapt to these variables. Make sure you're ready for your projects and take the time to complete them.

Don't Get Stuck

In addition to using fine mesh sheets on drying trays, as an additional insurance, I usually coat the sheets with a thin layer of cooking oil. Initially I used a non-stick cooking spray to cover the trays. Be careful to do it in the sink or on a tray that doesn't worry about getting fat. Spraying a tray or sheet in the air can create a slippery mess on the floor, something I have learned from experience. In the end, I decided to prefer to grease the trays with a paper napkin soaked in olive oil, a neutral oil such as rapeseed or grape seed or a sweet and tasty oil such as almond oil. It seemed less messy and avoided introducing propellants into our atmosphere.

There are also various accessories to be used alone or in addition to oil to prevent adhesion. For example, if you are preparing minced meat with minced meat or if you want to prepare small individual portions of fruit skin, you can buy coated paper strips about 7.5 cm wide, which can be used in the round or rectangular dehydrators

Commercial dryers can have stainless steel trays, whose food tends to stick more than the non-stick plastic versions. For this type of dryer, you need to be very careful when greasing the trays and you will probably want to invest in non-stick sheets of fruit netting and / or fruit skin sheets to be placed on top of steel for smaller or more liquid objects.

Choose the Right Point for the Dehydrator

My dehydrators live in the basement. This is somewhat inconvenient, since I often have to run downstairs with uncomfortable trays, for example of grapes that threaten to fall at any time. But the dehydrators are a bit noisy; they make almost the same amount of noise as a kitchen hood. Depending on what you're drying, they can also smell. If you're drying out a batch of pineapples, the whole room may have a fragrant smell like a tropical tiki bar, but if you're making homemade garlic powder, you may not want to dehydrate nearby. So if you can place your dehydrator in a place other than your main living / sleeping area, we recommend that you do so. If you choose to put it in a cellar or garage, make sure the area is clean and dry.

Choose the Right Food

Select only foods in good shape to dry. Dehydration will not improve foods that have passed their peak. I make sure to dry myself with the seasons, buying large quantities of fresh, solid and attractive ingredients as they appear in the markets, and making sure that they are not dented or hide errors or rot.

Frozen fruits and vegetables can also be dried, either as part of a fruit peel puree, or individually if the objects are small, such as berries or corn kernels. If you don't have the time or the tendency to dry your fresh fruit from the market in mid-summer, you can freeze it on baking trays before transferring it to the freezer bags for longer storage (and then dehydrating it later if you wish).

Food Preparation for Drying

Wash and dry fruit or vegetables before dehydrating them. For fresh garden food, also be careful to select any damaged products and unwanted sheets, stems or insects before drying.

Wash the food in a water bath. Strain and dry with a salad spinner if necessary, or place it on a clean tea towel to absorb moisture from the surface.

Space of Food Items in Trays

When placing foods on the drying trays, leave enough room for them to dry evenly. Slicing the ingredients evenly also helps to unify the drying time for a certain type of food. In recipes, I don't provide a specific number of trays to use for each product, as different dehydrators have different sizes, but keep in mind that you will get faster and more uniform drying if you put your ingredients in a single layer, leaving a good perimeter of the space, at least 1/2 inch [1 cm], between food bites. In general, I recommend preparing two trays, positioning the ingredients and then proceeding with more trays, if necessary. Also take some time to rotate the trays during drying to ensure the most uniform drying conditions; some dehydrator manuals say that this is not necessary, but it is better to do it. Follow the recommendations of your dehydrator regarding the minimum number of trays to be inserted in the dryer, even if not all of them contain ingredients.

When Done!

Dry foods can have many different textures and as you use your dehydrator more, you will learn how to measure the correct consistency. The dehydration table for common foods and recipes provides approximate drying times for various foods and also provides textual descriptions so you can decide for yourself when foods are produced. A piece of shots should be dry, opaque, but still a little flexible when ready; a sprig of basil should be completely dry and fresh. Since sugar is hydrophilic (tends to bind with water), foods with sugar in them tend to take longer to dry and may not become completely crunchy, hence the apparent chewiness of raisins or dried apricots. Therefore, if you add sugar or other sweeteners to the food you are drying, such as Foster Trail Banana Mix or Dried Cranberries, keep in mind that it will increase the drying time.

The good news is that although dehydration takes time, from about 3 hours for breadcrumbs and some herbs to 3 days for chillies or dried figs, the dehydration process does not require much active participation. Let's say you're waiting for some fruit to dry and take longer than expected. You watched television at night, but you really want to go to sleep. Don't get discouraged! If your project is not completely dry, you can turn off the dehydrator at night and restart it in the morning. Its ingredients may have dried properly with residual evaporation overnight. If not, turn the dryer back on.
Alternatively, you can lower the heat for dehydration overnight. This type of slow drying is particularly effective when you want to minimize the hardness of the food surface; you don't want a fig, for example, leathery on the outside but still completely moist and soft on the inside.

If You Go Too Far
It is possible to dry plums or tomatoes until they are too difficult to chew easily. If so, don't panic. You can place dry food on top of the stove in a saucepan equipped with a basket or a steaming basket on about 5 cm of boiling water. Steam for 5-10 minutes until softened to your preferred consistency. Or you can place the object in a suitable microwave container with 2-3 tablespoons of water, cover it safely and microwave in 30 second bursts until the food has softened.

Cleaning Up
Cleaning trays can sometimes be a challenge and an advantage of metal dehydrators is that their stainless steel trays are dishwasher safe. Although not recommended by the manufacturer, I confess that I often put my plastic drying trays in the dishwasher, in the quick setting, which does not overheat the plastic

in the drying cycle. But with warm soapy water and a stiff brush, it doesn't take long to clean the trays by hand, which is the best solution for long-lasting dehydration trays.

Storage for Results

Since the recipes in this book do not use artificial preservatives, the shelf life of dry foods may not be as long as that of commercially dried products. In general, I recommend eating what you dry within two weeks of placement, but that's not a strict rule. If you are drying wet fruit or vegetables for later use, then it is a good idea to condition your ingredients before permanent packaging. Dry foods keep well in airtight containers in a dark environment (such as a cupboard) at room temperature or cool. Including a pack of silica gel along with dry foods will prolong freshness. If you really want to extend the life of your dry foods, you can always put them in the freezer. It works well with more humid foods, as crunchy dry foods can lose consistency in the refrigerator or freezer.

Throughout the book, I will give you conservative estimates of the storage times of some dehydrated foods. Don't automatically throw food away at the end of my quote. I'm giving you tips on the ideal timeline for eating your dry food, not necessarily how long it will be edible. I advise you to use your observations to judge if your dry food is in good condition. Here are some tips for assessing the condition of stored dry food.

Strange smells and tastes: if dry food has a bad smell or taste, especially for dry meat, it has become rancid or moldy.

Sweatiness: If too much moisture builds up in the food container after the first two or three days of storage (when humidity levels may drop), it is possible that it will deteriorate. Put this dry food in the refrigerator or freezer.

Mold: mold is a clear sign of deterioration. I tend to throw the whole lot away only if I see it's moldy all over the place. If I only see one bad fruit, I throw it away and carefully check the rest of the lot.

Loss of Taste: the taste may come out of dry food after a while, especially if the food is not stored in the dark. This is more likely to happen with herbs, garlic and other powders. Once done, mix and create a new batch.

Dipping

It is not necessary to pre-treat the food before drying it. However, some elements, such as apples or peaches, turn brown due to exposure to oxygen on their cut surfaces and become less brown during drying when immersed in a solution of citric acid, which is the powdered form. of the acid found in lemon juice. (I chose not to use sodium bisulfate, the additive that preserves the color in many commercially dried fruits, as some people are allergic to it.) You can get citric acid in many health food stores and pharmacies, or online. When preparing a batch of such foods for drying, prepare a solution of 1 teaspoon of citric acid for every 9 qt [960 ml] of water in a large bowl, then drop the food and dip it for a couple of minutes. Drain as much as possible and place it in the prepared trays. Or you can use a one-to-one ratio of lemon juice and water, but this requires a lot of lemons!

Blanching

Bleaching is the process of short immersion of food in boiling water to stop the enzymatic actions that can cause loss of taste, color and consistency. After bleaching, the ingredients must be removed in an ice water bath to quickly stop cooking. This method is useful for various foods. For example, if blanched, spinach and young herbs retain their bright green color and dry faster. The process breaks the waxy skins of hard-skinned fruits such as grapes, blueberries, tomatoes, figs and blueberries and exposes the flesh of the fruit to the air circulating in the dehydrator. You can also use a basket for steaming food.

Conditioning

When drying the foods you want to be semi-selfish (such as gummy dried fruit), some pieces will retain more moisture than others. Before sealing them for long-term storage, you can take a step called conditioning to equalize moisture. Put some of the dry and cooled objects in an airtight jar and shake them every day for 5-6 days. Look for a significant accumulation of moisture in the container; If you see it, you may need to return the food to the dehydrator. After a period of conditioning, the food should be uniformly moist. So you can seal it very well, preferably with a silica gel pack to prolong the freshness.

Rehydrating

You can rehydrate most dry foods by placing them in a bowl, covering them with boiling water and soaking them for about 15 minutes. Depending on the food, you may want to incorporate the soaking liquid into the finished dish (for example, the mushroom soaking liquid can be used as a broth on the dish). You can also use a vaporizer to rehydrate food.

"Drying is a method for preserving food products in which so much natural moisture is removed from the product that the decomposing microorganisms (yeasts, molds and bacteria), even if present in living conditions, cannot grow or multiply.

"The process is not new, but the method is; the process is as old as bees. Bees collect nectar from flowers and store it in small cells where drones or workers keep a warm air flow over them. Warm air removes moisture leaving honey concentrated.

"Since the beginning of time, man has cured (dried) hay and grass, corn, herbs and meat for human and animal consumption thanks to the heat of the sun. Today in food storage, we achieve this cure or drying by evaporating moisture or water in food products from a liquid to a vapor. For this purpose, heat and air are needed, but the heat must be kept at a temperature that does not affect the consistency, color, taste or nutritional value of the product.

"The heat evaporates the water from the product and the air circulating around it absorbs the steam. Drying changes the appearance of the products, but if properly dried and preserved, very few original food nutrients are lost.

"Drying has the great advantage of minimizing storage problems. The weight of the dry product is from a quarter to a tenth, or in some cases even lower, compared to the fresh product. In addition, it can be stored almost indefinitely, if stored in the right conditions. "

Dehydrating Keeps Nutritional Values

Fresh fruit and vegetables are the richest sources of vitamins, minerals, sugars, proteins and other essential nutrients for good health. How necessary it is, therefore, that we do everything possible to conserve these nutrients. Although harvested or harvested, fruit and vegetables are still living materials capable of carrying out their life processes. After the product has been removed from its source of life, these processes, if left unchecked, destroy quality because they include the oxidation of precious materials within the product.

"The chemical changes that compromise the quality of the product, as well as the attacks by decomposing organisms, can be delayed by keeping the products in the refrigerator until they are processed, but this conservation should be as short as possible; two days should be the maximum time.

"Only products in excellent condition need to be dried, which means they must dry to the fullest when they have reached maturity and are fresh in the garden. Dehydrated fruits and vegetables that have been reconstituted and cooked provide approximately the same amount of carbohydrates, fats, proteins, minerals and mass as the original fresh material prepared in the same way. The proteins and minerals in dehydrated foods after reconstitution are no different from those of the original food if dehydrated at the correct recommended temperature. Since steamed vegetables help retain more nutrients than bleaching, we recommend following the instructions in the section on dehydrating vegetables.

"Fruits and vegetables not only provide important food nutrients, but also contribute to the normal functioning of the body. Fruits, with the exception of blueberries, plums and prunes; Vegetables, with the exception of rhubarb, spinach and chard, have an effect alkaline when oxidized in the body. Free acids and acid salts of fruits and vegetables are oxidized to carbonic acid which is removed by breathing. Vegetables provide salts of the metals calcium, magnesium, potassium and sodium, which are available for the purpose of neutralizing the acid from products derived from the protein metabolism of meat, eggs, milk and cereals. This is just one of the many reasons why a diet should include fruit and vegetables."

Fruits are an excellent source of vitamins A and C, but they are not very rich in vitamin B-1 (thiamine). Although sulfuring destroys vitamin B-1 in fruits, it tends to retain the potency of vitamins A and C. It is always best to keep most of the vitamins.

"Thiamine is well preserved in vegetables that have been steamed and steaming will help preserve part of the vitamin C in vegetables, which unfortunately is easily destroyed. Vitamin B-2 (riboflavin), present in some fruits and in many vegetables, it is resistant to oxidation, heat and sulfur fumes, but is influenced by light ... Niacin ... occurs in a few vegetables. It is not destroyed by oxidation or by heating to boiling temperature, so there should be a small loss of niacin in the dehydration process."

It is clear that dehydrated fruits and vegetables maintain almost all the nutritional values that foods have when they are fresh.

Metabolic Considerations Related To Dehydrated Food

Dehydrated foods are now of particular interest to the general public and can have a significant clinical application for those with blood sugar symptoms. Medical science has established that all cells in the body require an adequate balance of oxygen and various nutrients to facilitate the vital process of physiological combustion, which in turn provides the energy and metabolic elements necessary to maintain good health. .

The petrol engine is a dramatic example of the principle in question: it is well known that excess fuel "suffocates" the engine and very little "starves". The blood sugar in the body is comparable to motor gasoline and is the simplified digested sugar that is directly available to the cells for combustion. If the blood sugar level is too high, adequate combustion does not occur and a hyperglycemic or diabetic condition may prevail. If it is too low, a hypoglycemic condition or so-called "low blood sugar" can occur and cause unwanted clinical symptoms. Therefore, it is essential for good health that an adequate ratio of oxygen and blood sugar is available to provide ideal circumstances for the most important physiological combustion.

When natural foods are consumed and subjected to normal digestive processes, blood sugar gradually increases, maintains a longer effective maximum level and then gradually decreases to a level that indicates the need for additional nutrition. In contrast, sweeter and highly concentrated foods tend to increase blood sugar much faster, rush hour is shorter and lowering is generally much faster and can be followed by unwanted clinical symptoms.

The type of diet that people eat plays a huge role in the body's correct metabolism. Ideally, more natural foods provide the best sources of energy and nutrients for tissue building. Super sweet and highly concentrated foods often cause unwanted physiological problems. Dehydrated foods provide an excellent source of natural nutrition and should be considered in any realistic diet.

If prepared in the right way, these foods are very tasty, very tasty and provide excellent nutritional values without the excessive stress of overeating. Many people have noticed that eating very small portions of dehydrated food satisfies the feeling of hunger and produces high energy returns. Another interesting feature is the fact that, when prepared according to the instructions, these foods can be stored in a relatively small space at room temperature, offering a definitive storage advantage.

In conclusion, it can be empirically stated that the intake, digestion, metabolism and subsequent physiological functions of the body are much better with more natural foods. Therefore, dehydrated foods offer some very definite and desirable benefits and may very well occupy a different place in the medical world of good nutrition.

PART 2

CHAPTER FOUR - FOOD DEHYDRATION METHODS

Different methods have been used to dehydrate fruits and vegetables. Each has its advantages and disadvantages and you should study them carefully to decide which method best suits your family's needs. The needs of a family that will dehydrate some elements in small quantities during the year are obviously different from those of a large family that will dehydrate bushels of different types of fruit, vegetables and meat.

Method 1: Solar Drying

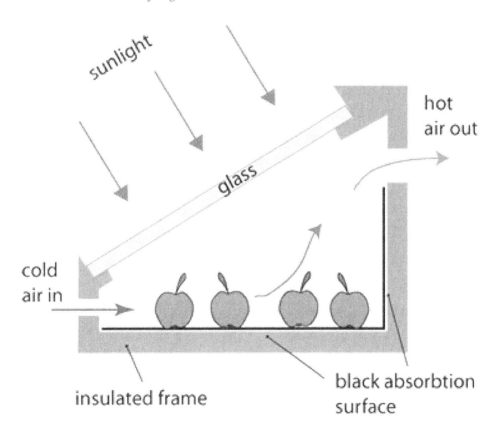

"This method is perhaps the oldest known method of preserving food. It is the evaporation of water from the products by solar or solar heat, supported by the movements of the surrounding air. The products are distributed in containers of one type or another (such as the window screen) that tilt south to receive the full effect of direct sunlight.

An example is a sun dried tomatoes.
"Drying in the sun is not the most satisfying method. To be successful, it requires a season without bright sunshine and high temperatures, coinciding with a period of maturity of fruit and vegetables. Drying in the sun requires considerable care. I products must be protected from insects with a screen or a net and must be taken to a shelter when blowing dust or raining and before the dew falls at night. If there is no succession of sunny days, there is a danger of deterioration. At best this method is slow because the sun does not cause rapid evaporation of moisture.
"Before storage, sun dried products must be placed in an artificial heat dryer for 20-30 minutes. This will complete drying and destroy all bacteria that may have accumulated during the drying process. "

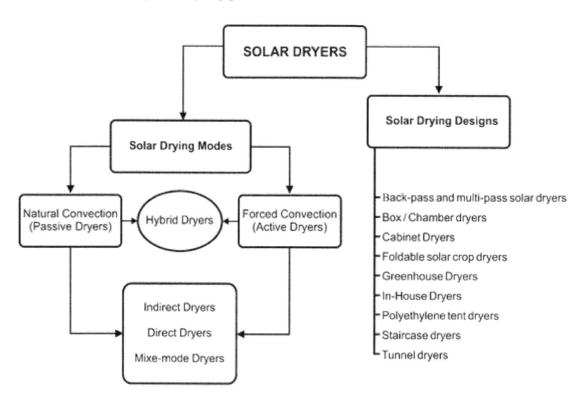

Artificial heat during drying, such as that found in a well-designed dehydrator, has many advantages compared to drying in the sun: it can be used regardless of weather conditions, it is ready to work when the product is mature, it can be controlled, it can being continuous, it is a faster process, the products retain their natural color better and the flavor and nutrients are preserved to a much greater extent.

Method 2: Use of a Net Bag

Food can be prepared and placed in a mesh bag and hung on the laundry. Again, the advantage of this method is that it requires very little investment and keeps insects and birds away. However, the bag must be carried every night and every time it rains and the bag must be shaken regularly to redistribute the food so that it dries completely and evenly. It will work, but it is obviously a limited method and sheets a lot to be desired.

 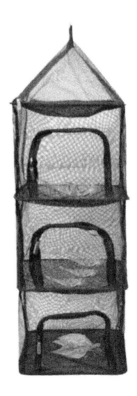

Method 3: Oven Drying

Fruits and vegetables can be dried in the oven. The kitchen must be well ventilated and be careful to keep the heat low. Set the regulator to 140-145 ° F and preheat the oven. When the product is first placed in the oven, the temperature will drop, but will soon build up. Do not allow the temperature to rise above 145 ° F.

When drying fruit or vegetables in an electric oven, leave the door two inches open. When using a gas oven, the door must be open eight inches. This helps control the temperature, but it is also necessary to allow moisture to escape through air circulation.

"If an oven with a regulator is not available, a portable oven thermometer is a great convenience, although you can learn from the" feel "of the product if it is drying satisfactorily or not. It should feel moist and slightly cooler than the air flowing over it. Otherwise, it is drying too fast. "

Food can be placed in pans or trays; Open mesh trays speed up the drying process. Tray frames can be made of either 1/2 or 1/2 inch wood. The frames must be small enough to fit on the oven racks. Cover the frames with any open mesh material such as curtain net, cheese cloth, muslin or sturdy washable nylon net. If necessary, reinforce the deck by stretching the strings diagonally across the frame below. This will prevent tissue relaxation. Distribute the prepared product on the trays in a deep layer and place the trays on the oven shelves. Mix the product and rotate the trays from time to time to ensure uniform drying.

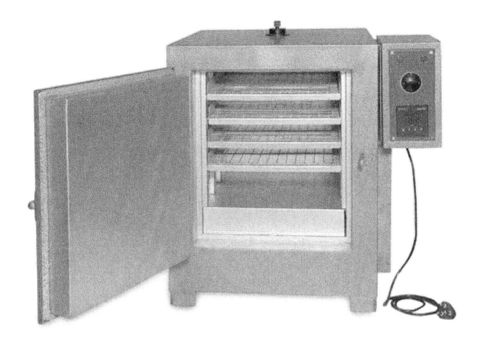

The disadvantages of drying the oven are many: it is difficult to get enough air movement, it can be difficult to get a low enough temperature in the oven to preserve nutrients and color, two racks are not efficient when large quantities are dehydrated, and the oven is off. is now not available for any other use.

Method 4: Dehydrators

HOMEMADE:

Building a domestic dehydrator that produces end products of the highest quality is a very difficult task for maintenance personnel.

1. Box with wooden frame
A dehydrator can be built from a wooden box in which an electric heating element or a gas burner and a fan have been installed. This provides better control of temperature and air movement, but becomes difficult to clean and can absorb odors from food. Considerable experimentation is needed to obtain the correct

movement and air temperature in the domestic units to obtain optimal drying conditions.

2. Refrigerator

An old refrigerator can be used to make a dehydrator by adding a fan, shelf supports and a heating element. This provides more control and is easier to clean, but requires some skill with sheet metal processing and requires experimentation to achieve the correct temperature and air movement. It is also very cumbersome for the space used and is difficult to store or move.

COMMERCIAL BUILT UNITS:

1. Speed: "Whatever the drying method, in the sun or with controlled heat, speed is the word to keep in mind, both when preparing fresh food to be dried and when starting the drying process. The faster you work, the higher the vitamin value of dry foods and the better the color, flavor and quality of cooking. "

2. Temperature: authorities recommend a maintained temperature of 140–145 ° F in cabinet dryers. If the temperature is too low, the food can become acidic and

spoil. Dr. D.K. Salunkhe of Utah State University says that dehydrated food at 160 ° F will lose three times more vitamins than dehydrated food at 140-145 ° F.

The drying and cracking of the surface is avoided by controlling the temperature and the air flow. The right temperature is obviously obtained by increasing or decreasing the heat source. If controlled by a thermostatically controlled heat source, the temperature should remain fairly constant in the loaded operating cabinet. When the products start to dry for the first time, there is little risk of burns, but when they are almost dry, they burn easily (and abrasion destroys the taste and nutritional value).

3. Air circulation: when the static air has absorbed all the humidity it can retain, there can be no further evaporation from a wet object. Therefore, measures must be taken to remove the moist air and replace it with dry air so that evaporation can continue. "However, if the moisture on the surface evaporates faster than the internal fabrics spread it on the surface, the surface hardens, the internal moisture cannot pass, and drying is delayed. This surface drying is called "case hardening". In the well-designed dehydrator, an air-cooled fan achieves adequate air circulation.

"Drying is best achieved when the process is continuous because the growth of microorganisms is reduced to a minimum, while when the heat is applied intermittently, temperatures favorable to bacterial growth can develop."

4. Comfort: the various racks offer greater drying capacity. Dehydration can be achieved at night. It is not necessary to place the unit in an area that requires ventilation. We dehydrated the food in our basement, for example, without appreciable differences in humidity.

Root vegetables, such as carrots, potatoes, onions and cabbage, can be stored in a basement until the winter season and can therefore be dehydrated at your convenience. However, when vegetables such as carrots and potatoes are stored for a long period of time, the starch in the vegetables turns into sugar and this condition prolongs the dehydration time by an appreciable amount.

Method 5: Preservatives

Many people don't want to use preservatives of any kind. If you plan to dehydrate the fruit for a short storage period (i.e. six to nine months), you don't need preservatives. However, if you plan to store fruit for a longer period of time, you need to use some form of preservative. This preserves the color and decreases the loss of vitamins and, therefore, preserves the nutritional value of the food.

The method of preserving vegetables by bleaching is discussed in the section on dehydrating vegetables.

One method of preserving the color and flavor of natural fruit is to immerse the fruit in one of the following solutions:

Erythrobic acid or ascorbic acid: soak the fruit for two minutes only in a solution of a spoonful of erythrobic acid or ascorbic acid dissolved in a gallon of water. This preparation delays oxidation and prevents darkening of light colored fruits during the dehydration process.

Sodium bisulfite solution: soak the fruit for two minutes only in a solution of one tablespoon of sodium bisulfite in one liter of water. Sodium bisulphite helps prevent darkening of the fruit during the storage period. Drain well.

Combination of sodium bisulfite and ascorbic or erythorbic acid: another method is to use a combination of a spoonful of sodium bisulfite and a spoonful of erythrobic acid or ascorbic acid dissolved in a gallon of water. This method preserves the quality and color during the dehydration process and during the storage period. If you plan to dry your fruit in the sun, it should definitely be sulfur because the heat source is uncontrolled and constant. However, if the fruit is dried in a well-designed dehydrator in which this heat source is controlled and constant, less oxidation occurs and the fruit retains more of its color.

For those who are concerned about the intake of sulfur in the human body, Dr. D. K. Salunkhe of Utah State University says, "The body needs sulfur, which is part of a certain type of protein." Moderate exposure of fruits to sulfur fumes (as described below) is certainly beneficial for the product when using an intermittent heat source and is not toxic to the health of consumers. The heat of drying and subsequent cooking dissipates practically all the sulfur.

Another method of preserving the color and flavor of natural fruit in fruit is by sulfidating the compartment. "It can be a box, as long as it is large enough to cover the trays and a sulfur tray. The sulfur tray can be any shallow tray or metal lid, such as a baking powder lid. A packing box can be covered with roofing paper or canvas, or it is possible to build a compartment with panels or cardboard boxes. A small opening should be provided near the bottom of the container for ventilation. Sulfur will not burn without it. All sulfuring must be done outdoors; The opening should be closed after all the sulfur has burned to retain the fumes long enough to "cure" the product.

Choosing a Dehydrator

You can test your first dehydration experiments in a domestic oven, setting it to the lowest possible temperature (preferably with the convection fan on, if your oven has that function). Improvise a drying rack by placing a cooling rack on a baking sheet. With this approach, food will dry faster than a dehydrator and can be crunchy in places, but it's a fun way to get started. Soon, however, you will likely want to invest in a home dehydrator, which will provide greater control and even results.

Domestic dehydrators combine a circulation fan with heating elements to heat food from about 35 ° to 74 ° C [95 ° to 165 ° F]. Inside, they have multiple layered trays in plastic or metal that allows hot air to circulate around the food and speed up evaporation, so the food dries uniformly without gilding too much.
You will need a dehydrator with adjustable temperature control and I really appreciate having a timer on the machine. Since dehydration takes a long time, it is useful to turn off the machine at 2 am instead of having to do it.

Stackable Dehydrators

The most used food dehydrators are round and stackable benchtop machines. In this variant, the fan and heating unit are located on top of a pile of donut-shaped trays that fill with ready-to-dry foods. Hot air flows around the perimeter of the trays and through the food in the trays. A drip tray on the bottom captures all the juices. Nesco is the most popular manufacturer of this type of dehydrator. Smaller units, which are about the size of a large cake box, are relatively inexpensive. These models have several advantages: they are small and light. The capacity of the machine can be increased simply by purchasing additional stacking trays (the manufacturer's instructions indicate the number of trays that can be used in relation to the power of the dehydrator drying unit). Trays have pronounced edges, so foods with polyethylene rolls like cherry tomatoes do not roll up as you transport them. Accessories such as fruit drying sheets in leather and net drying sheets are cheap and easy to obtain; they also have a lip on them, to hold liquid foods like soup or ketchup. And the stackable trays are small and relatively easy to clean. Although it is not officially sanctioned, I will slide the sticky trays through the dishwasher in a quick setting to get a really complete wash, but you should avoid the hot drying cycle.

The downside of these round stackers is the donut shape of the trays, which doesn't offer much drying area. And if you're making fruit skin, it's difficult to evenly distribute the fruit on these trays and cut it into regular pieces.

Rectangular Box Dehydrators

If you want to increase the price, you will find rectangular box dehydrators with completely removable trays (the most common brand is Excalibur). They take up more space in your kitchen (they are the size of a small but lighter microwave oven) and their capacity is established; the most common model has nine trays, although larger and larger units are available. Individual rectangular trays can hold more food than donut-shaped trays, which is great if you work with ingredients like orange slices or fennel slices. If you are making a fruit skin, the rectangular lot can easily be cut into uniform strips.

These box-shaped machines have the fan / heater unit on the back, so there is no need to lift the unit while turning the trays or pulling out a finished batch (as with the stackable round dehydrator). This design also offers a more uniform heat distribution throughout the machine, so there is no need to rotate the trays as much. (But as the heat increases, you still need to rotate the trays at least once during the drying process for consistent results.)

Excalibur dryers also have a fluctuating heat cycle during operation instead of the continuous cycle present in other dryers. When the temperature cools slightly during drying, the manufacturer claims that the internal humidity shifts outward. And when the heat rises again, the external moisture evaporates at a faster rate. In theory, this minimizes hardening during drying.

In the Excalibur basic system, the trays are made of plastic with inlays with thin polyethylene meshes that prevent the berries from falling. (In circular tray systems, the holes are larger, although finer mesh liner sheets can be purchased for smaller items.) Mesh inlays are useful because you can roll them up while unloading food into a container, channelling all loose pieces without getting them dirty.

Polyethylene mesh screens are not made for disinfecting at high temperatures, which you may want to do if you are working in spurts. Stainless steel dehydrators with metal trays are available, which can be boiled or steamed to facilitate the cleaning process, but are more expensive. These heavy-duty steel machines are heavier than plastic models.

If you are creating an activity, you can consider all types of dehydrator updates: higher volume machines, those with two temperature zones and, of course, freeze drying units that make the food fresh and dry almost instantly. But the car-level price on some of these machines is too much for most home users.

Accessories and Tools

Like all good hobbies, dehydrating food can lead you to want to use some serious accessories and tools, some more crucial than others. You don't need everything on this list to get started, but these items have served me well in my dehydrating kitchen.

Airtight Containers

Once you start to dehydrate, you will begin to collect containers to store dehydrated food. You can never have enough.

Mason, Bell and Weck cans are an attractive way to store your dry products. And glass is recommended for storing acidic foods. You will be tempted to show your dry items in the kitchen window, but they will last longer if stored in a dark closet. Spice jars are perfect for powdered foods. The best ones have an airtight rubber or silicone seal on the lid.

Vacuum bag systems are very effective for packaging because they are heat sealed and automatically remove additional air before sealing.

Plastic freezer bags (and small ones for backpacks) are effective and easy to use and are compactly stored. Press the extra air from each bag to stack it.

Blender

A large blender, especially a high-speed, high-capacity blender (such as a Vitamix), can quickly blend and spray dry powdered ingredients.

Caramel Thermometer

I use a method of hot sugar syrup for my dehydrating meringues, which is much easier to do with a thermometer adapted for very hot environments. You should be able to find a candy thermometer in your hallway, in kitchen shops or online.

Cherry Pitter

You really only need a cherry pitter if you plan to dry the cherries (or maybe olives); If this is your plan, you will be happy to have one. I use a small portable model that looks a bit like a stapler; but if you really make a lot of cherries, you can look for a lever cherry picker on the counter (or Cherry Stoner).

Food Mill

A crank feeder is a useful low-tech tool for making soft passes for fruit and vegetable skins, especially if you want a finer texture. The screen at the bottom separates the hard hides and large seeds from the pulp, making a puree very smooth.

Food Processor

A large food processor can come in handy in the home dehydration kitchen. With large motor and sharp blades, you can cut meat, slice or destroy vegetables almost instantly, dry powdered ingredients and fruit puree. However, it is less convenient to grind, cut or whisk small batches.

Jerky Gun

This specialized tool is used to jerk minced meat and is particularly useful for producing a large quantity. I find it practical and fun. An irregular gun works like a caulking gun; extrude the seasoned meat onto the non-stick sheets in clean ribbons or cylinders. For this purpose, you can also use a dedicated pastry bag with a flat tip.

Mandoline

Basically a flat tool with a sharp cutting edge running through the center, a mandolin is a fantastic and easy-to-clean tool for evenly cutting fruit and vegetables. Cheap plastic models are good for items like cucumbers, apples, pears, onions and fennel.
I like the V-shaped blade of the uniform cut of the Swissmar Borner mandolin. Sturdy metal mandolins such as the Bron slicer are ideal for sticky and starchy vegetables such as potatoes, sweet potatoes and celery root. When using a mandolin, remember to use the fingertip protection provided with the instrument so as not to cut the fingertips.

Microplanes and Other Graters

Scraper-type graters, such as a Microplane, produce thin grated shavings of fresh citrus or cheese that will dry quickly in the dehydrator. The thin holes in a box grater also work well, but make sure the grater is still sharp (otherwise it may be time to replace it).

Nonstick Fruit Leather Sheets

If you work with sticky foods such as fruit peels, you will need to stock up on lining sheets for the dehydrator trays. Do not use wax paper; it will crumble in the drying process. If you work with a Nesco-style round dehydrator, you can purchase additional leather sheets to cover the trays. These are super soft donut-shaped plastic discs that can hold liquid or semi-liquid foods such as fruit purees or soups while you dry them. If you work with a square dryer Excalibur produces excellent sheets with ParaFlexx coating that adapt to the screens in polyethylene mesh on the trays. You can also use the strongest silicone mats, such as the Silpat brand, for the same purpose; just make sure the mats are the right size for your trays. It is also useful to keep one of these non-stick sheets on the bottom of the dehydrator to facilitate cleaning of the machine.

Non-Adhesive Mesh Sheets

Most stacked round dryers come with additional mesh sheets, but in the end you will want to get some more from these easy-to-clean screens, which line up the trays and prevent small pieces of food from falling through the holes. If you buy an Excalibur-style square dehydrator, which comes with trays already lined with polyethylene mesh screens, you may want to purchase some additional screens.

Notebook and Pen

You will need to record the time and temperature of your drying projects so that you can better customize your dehydrator based on your climate and techniques. I like to keep the laptop on top of the dehydrator, so if I add some extra drying time to a project, I don't forget to record it.

Offset Spatula

This pastry tool is really useful if you are producing a lot of fruit peels and you need to distribute the purees in an orderly and uniform way.

Peelers

Peelings are ideal for both skin removal and for thin and easy to dehydrate strips of lemon peel, asparagus, carrots and parsnips. I am in favor of the Y-shaped potato peelers and replace them every year or two, so they are always sharp enough to make my bet.

Ruler

If you want the jerky or apple slices to dry as evenly as possible, keep a small ruler on the tools to make sure you cut or evenly form the elements before processing.

Short Brush

This tool is essential for cleaning screens and dehydrator trays. I also use a pot washing brush and a short, flexible toothbrush-shaped brush to get rid of cracks and crevices.

Silica Gel Packages

These mysterious little packages are often in the pack when you buy a new pair of shoes. They are full of silica crystals that absorb moisture. They are particularly useful for preventing the accumulation of dust and preventing mold. I started to accumulate them from the packages I found them in and now I order them online. There are also oxygen absorbent packs on the market that further extend the shelf life of dry foods, but their use is more complicated. If you are deeply involved in the long-term storage of your dry foods, you may want to get to know them.

Spice Grinder

The only tool you will find indispensable for preparing food for dehydration is a coffee grinder. My coffee grinder is actually an inexpensive coffee grinder dedicated to the use of spices. Its small size and fast-rotating sharp blades are ideal for small batches of light ingredients. But if you don't have a coffee grinder and find a recipe that requires one, you can use other tools such as a mortar, blender or food processor.

Spider

A spider is a long-handled tool with a large wire mesh shovel at the end. It is my favorite tool for fishing for bleach items in a hot water pot. They are inexpensive and can be found in Asian markets, in kitchenware stores or online. You can also use a spoon or a large-cut strainer to complete the job.

Steamer

Although it is possible to use a large pot of boiling water to blanch vegetables and fruit before dehydrating them, steam is also an effective method.

Timer

It can be very useful to have more than one timer on hand while it is drying. You can keep track of your drying time in one near the dehydrator and take another one with you if you walk away from the machine and need a reminder to turn it off at a specific time.

PART 3

CHAPTER FIVE - DEHYDRATING FRUIT

Dried fruit is sweet of nature, but unlike sweet, it retains most of the vitamins, minerals and fibers inherent in the fruit, making it more nutritious and abundant. I stick to a caveman type diet, so chocolate bars are available for me, but dried fruit (in modest quantities) is inside. Dried fruits retain the minerals, caloric content and fiber found in fresh fruit.

They also retain most of the niacin, thiamine, vitamin A and riboflavin from fresh fruit. The only vitamin that undergoes significant loss during dehydration is vitamin C and the fruits lose 90% or more of their vitamin C during dehydration.

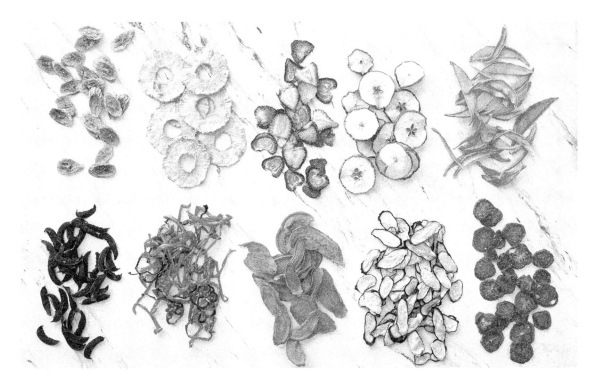

This effect can be slightly improved by choosing to pre-treat the fruit with ascorbic acid before dehydrating it.

Dried fruit is a healthier sweet snack than most you can buy in the snack aisle, but dried fruit (other than raisins) that you can buy at the store tends to be so incredibly expensive that it is really good. Since I don't have a driver to accompany me to the Rolls-Royce grocery store, nor a personal buyer to take care of me, I usually make my nuts for a better product at a lower price.

Dried fruits are fantastic and are also good additions to cereal, fruit and nut blends and cake recipes. You can also spray dried fruit, mix them with hot water and reconstitute them in a consistency similar to apple sauce. A little-known use for dried fruit is the production of country wines.

Dried fruit provides sugar, but gives sherry a different and pleasant character when added during the primary fermentation phase of the country's wines.

Much of my dried fruit comes from apples, pears and vines, but I also buy bananas, pineapples, peaches and other fruits in supermarkets and farm stalls.

Sometimes I buy more than I can use before it goes wrong, or I have just a difficult week at work and I'm not at home as expected, so I don't eat all the fruit I expected.

Anyway, I end up with a fruit that will go wrong unless you do something about it. More often than not, this means breaking the dehydrator.

For apples, I have what must be the most ingenious invention in the world, even if I didn't invent it alone. It is a potato peeler that peels, cuts and shells the apple in seconds.

I have a robust model that has lasted for years. I once had an inexpensive version, but it broke after using it only a few times. For other fruits, I end up cutting by hand, but even so, the preparation takes only a couple of minutes.

Selecting Fruit for Dehydration

Any fruit can be dehydrated. The main question is whether dehydrating that particular fruit will give you the final product you want. Many citrus fruits and some melons contain so much water and so little cellulose structure that dehydration gives them bad results.

Likewise, the quality of the initial fruit is important. Although I have seen numerous tips on using only the highest quality fruit, this is not necessary. For example, I used apples infected with sooty mold (which does not penetrate under the skin and is unpleasant but harmless) to produce spectacular dried apples after peeling them. If so, dehydration provides a great way to use fruits that would otherwise not be tasty. Likewise, bananas that are just beyond the fresh feeding phase and turn brown but which are otherwise edible are a perfect candidate for dehydration. This way you are actually adding value.

But it is important that the fruit is healthy. By this I mean that it can't be something you don't eat fresh. I would like to eat the slightly ripe banana without hesitation. And I peeled and ate the soot of moldy apples on my skin. But I would not have eaten something rotten, internally infected with something or that had lost its structural integrity. Since I wouldn't eat those things, I wouldn't dehydrate them either because dehydrating them wouldn't improve them. You should also avoid unripe fruit. It is best to select ripe or slightly ripe fruit to dehydrate.

Most of the fruits are good candidates for the dehydrator. Apples, pears, plums, peaches, cherries, bananas, strawberries and even kiwis can dehydrate with excellent results.

Preparing Fruit

Fruits with hard or inedible grains must be cored or cut around the core so that they can be discarded. Apples and pears, especially pears, work best if peeled before cutting them into ¼ "slices. Remove the pits from all the stone fruits (peaches, cherries, etc.)

It is not necessary to peel stone fruits, such as prunes or nectarines, but they retain better and dehydrate more quickly if they are immersed whole in boiling water for two or three seconds before cutting them in half and removing the stones.

Once immersed in boiling water, the skin immediately slips if you want to remove it. The berries can be dehydrated in half with the cut side facing down on the dehydration tray.

Fruits such as grapes, blueberries, cherries and figs have a waxy coating which makes dehydration difficult. You can break the skins by placing them in a wire basket, immersing them in boiling water for a couple of seconds, then immersing them in ice water.

After preparation, the fruit must be pretreated.

Pretreating Fruit

The fruit is pretreated mainly to inhibit oxidation during drying and storage, therefore it retains its original color, but also has other benefits. Pretreatment helps hard-skinned fruits, like grapes, to dry faster and last longer in storage. Furthermore, it makes the final product safer by reducing the populations of E. coli, salmonella and listeria.

Pretreatment is obtained by immersing the prepared fruit in a solution containing lemon juice, citric acid, ascorbic acid (also known as vitamin C) or metabisulfite for five minutes. For apples, pears, cherries, kiwis, bananas and grapes, I have had better results with vitamin C and citric acid. For stone fruits, such as apricots and plums, I have had better results with sodium metabisulfite.

Citric acid powder, ascorbic acid powder and sodium metabisulphite are available at a good price from equipment suppliers and beer stores that cater to home wine producers. The attached table shows the relative costs of a liter of pretreatment solution for the various options. As you can see, citric acid and metabisulfite are the most profitable options, with ascorbic acid as a runner-up and lemon juice as a rather outrageous approach.

Traditional Sulfuring

Sulfur has been used in winemaking and fruit preservation for centuries. The ancient Romans burned sulfur-infused candles in wine barrels to keep them free from decaying organisms.

The traditional method of sulfurization of the fruit consists in burning the sulfur flowers (a form of elemental sulfur in powder) in a limited space that contains the fruit. Wet fruit is stacked on the shelves and then a bell is placed on the shelves. The sulfur is placed under the shelves and ignites. The sulfur dioxide vapors produced by combustion combine with any humidity present to form a weak sulphurous acid. This acid combines with potassium and sodium compounds naturally available to form sulphites. The whole process takes only 3-4 minutes and hundreds of kilos of fruit can be handled simultaneously. Sulfites are antiseptics and antioxidants.

Although this method works, I don't recommend doing it at home because it's unnecessarily dangerous. The burning sulfur transforms into a mass of molten splashes which presents a fire hazard and could easily splash onto the skin. Of course, if you choose to do it, you should do it outdoors on a rocky surface with nothing flammable.

In addition, sulfur-burning vapors, if inhaled, combine with moisture in the lungs to form sulphurous acid1 and will act in a harmful way, similar to the results of inhaling the phosgene from a WWI gas attack. . When phosgene gas finds water in the lungs, it creates hydrochloric acid which combines with water to form hydrochloric acid. As you can imagine, a lung full of hydrochloric acid is a rather dangerous and life-threatening event. The sulfuric acid created in the lungs by breathing sulfur dioxide is as dangerous as the hydrochloric acid produced by the phosgene.

The U.S. Administration for Safety and Health at Work has established very strict guidelines on sulfur dioxide exposure because only 1/10 of 1% in a room's atmosphere can kill a person in ten minutes.

This is a very technical way of saying that although I have explained how sulfur the old way, you shouldn't use this method at home, and certainly not inside a house. If you do it and make a mistake, you could seriously injure yourself or kill yourself or others. Instead, you should use modern sulfiting methods with a solid safety record.

Modern Sulfiting

Sulphites are used everywhere in wine production and sanitation in cellars and in beer production equipment, and are commonly used in the production of nuts and for storing kosher sauerkraut. They prevent dried fruits from turning brown by inhibiting the polyphenol oxidase enzyme and converting the orthinquinones into diphenols.

They have been used in various aspects of fruit processing for over two thousand years.

Despite the long history of sulfite use, there are reports that some people are sensitive and react negatively to sulphites. Attempts to find out how widespread this sensitivity may have given widely divergent results ranging from 0.05% 2 of the population to 1% 3 of the population, with approximately 5% of people with sensitive asthma. Obviously, if you are sensitive to sulphites, you should not use them as a pretreatment. However, for everyone else, they are an excellent choice with a solid safety record.

Sulfite is generally available in three forms: sodium metabisulfite powder, potassium metabisulfite powder and Campden tablets containing previously measured amounts of sodium or potassium metabisulfite.

If you are making wine, the difference in atomic weight and the effects of flavor between the forms of sodium and potassium metabisulfite could make a difference in which you choose and how much you use to reach a certain concentration in parts per million. But when you use sulfites for fruit pretreatment, you don't have to be so precise.

You can mix a spoonful of any of the compounds (or 40-50 Campden tablets) with a liter of water and shake until it dissolves, then soak the fruits for five minutes before putting them in the dryer. You can buy two ounces of sodium metabisulfite, making it a very convenient pretreatment.

Citric Acid / Lemon Juice

Lemon juice will work as an antioxidant for fruits, but it needs a lot, as it is mixed with 50/50 water for effective pretreatment. Given the cost of lemons and the amount needed to prepare a cup of lemon juice, it's not a very profitable option unless you have a lemon tree, although the fact that it's 100% natural is really attractive. If I am doing some dehydration in a small batch, I will often squeeze a lemon into a bowl of water and use it.

The active ingredient in lemon juice is citric acid and citric acid can be purchased in powder form from home-made suppliers and also from many of the major retail websites. It is very cheap; You can buy two ounces of citric acid.

(It is even less expensive per unit if purchased in bulk.) Mix a teaspoon with a liter of water and pre-treat the fruit by immersing it in the solution for five minutes before placing it on the grill.

Citric acid is the least expensive pre-treatment option for fruit and works great on apples, pears and bananas, among other fruits. Citric acid is what gives lemonade its distinctive flavor and you may notice some of the flavor in the fruit you are dealing with, but it is generally not a problem. When the fruits are dehydrated, their sugars are concentrated, so the small amount of acidity imparted by the citric acid left in the fruit after it has been immersed is barely noticeable.

Ascorbic Acid / Vitamin C

Considering the crazy prices charged for some vitamin C tablets in stores, I think the use of ascorbic acid as a pre-treatment would be prohibitive, but nothing could be further from the truth. Companies that sell vitamin C pay for labels, brands, marketing campaigns, etc. But when you buy Vitamin C powder in an envelope from the home brew shop, it costs around $ 3.89 for two ounces (the equivalent of two hundred 500 mg tablets).

On the flip side, you have to use quite a bit to do an antioxidant pre-treatment. You need 2 and a half tablespoons mixed with a liter of water. High concentrations are needed because it is destroyed by the heat of the dehydrator. Although vitamin C is a more expensive pre-treatment option, if dehydrated fruit is one of the main sources of vitamin C in the diet, it is worth considering.

Dehydrating

With all foreplay, effective dehydration is easy. The three ingredients are temperature, air flow and time.

The water will migrate from an area where it is more concentrated to a place where it is less concentrated, assuming that there is a means for such migration. The air can retain more humidity at higher temperatures than at lower temperatures. As an extreme example, the amount of humidity required to provide 80% relative humidity at a temperature of 30 degrees will only provide a relative humidity of 17% at 72 degrees. Therefore, the warmer the air, the faster and more completely it will absorb moisture from the food that is being dehydrated.

Of course, you're trying to dehydrate food instead of cooking it, and the higher the temperature used, the more it will adversely affect the content of vitamins, especially vitamin C.

Therefore, the optimal dehydration temperatures represent a commitment to achieve faster dehydration without cooking and still keeping as many vitamins as possible. The optimal temperature to achieve this balance varies with dehydrated food, but for fruits it is between 120 and 135 degrees.

Air flow is needed to expel moisture-laden air and bring fresh, low humidity air. In modern dehydrators this is done with a fan, although it can also be done through a "chimney effect" because warm air is lighter than cold air and will naturally increase. Therefore, some dehydrators that do not have fans have air vents on the bottom for fresh air and air vents on the top to let out the hot air. In my experience, fans work faster, but I have had success with both projects.

Time is the final ingredient and the amount of time required depends on the dehydration temperature, the thickness of the cut fruit, the particular fruit that is dehydrated and the environmental humidity. In practice, this cannot be expected except in very inaccurate terms. It is best to simply store the fruit in the dehydrator and monitor it every two hours until it is ready.

Organize your prepared and pre-treated fruit on drying trays in a single layer without touching the edges. This will ensure complete drying. Once the fruit has been placed, place the trays in the dehydrator and turn it on, setting the temperature between 120 and 135 degrees Fahrenheit.

Modern dehydrators supply heat through an electric heating element and the movement of air through a fan. Since dehydration has been done in much of human history by putting food on the shelves in the sun, modern dehydrators may seem excessive, but this is not the case. The success of the old dehydration methods was largely dictated by luck: ambient temperature and humidity, rain and sun.

Somewhere like in New Hampshire, summer humidity levels are rarely below 80% and there are times when we don't see the sun for more than an hour or two during the day, so we dehydrate on the shelves in the sun it will rarely produce a product that is well preserved and does not model itself. In Arizona, traditional methods work much better.

What modern dehydrators offer you is the ability to create a constant quality product suitable for long-term storage, in which the humidity level of the product can be brought well below atmospheric humidity levels in a very short time without mold.

With experience, you will develop an eye for it, but until the eye develops, here are some ways to evaluate whether the fruits are dry enough. Take a piece of fruit and cut it in half.

Tighten as tight as you can near the broken edge. If it shows no signs of moisture near the tear, it's done. Another indication for most fruits (except plums, dates and raisins) is that they don't hold together. A final test is to take several hot pieces from the dehydrator and put them in a sealed bag (like a zippered sandwich bag) and then put the bag in the refrigerator. Come back in an hour and see if there is condensation inside the bag. In such a case, the fruit should be dried longer. If there is no condensation, it is already done.

There is nothing wrong, in my opinion, if the fruit dries too much. You know it's too dry when it's fragile. Too dried fruit seems to me an excellent snack for people who love crunchy things.

Specific Fruits

Apples and pears can be peeled or unpeeled. They must be washed and soulless. They can then be cut into quarters or cut from ¼ "to ⅜" and placed on the grid after pre-treatment. Citric acid works best as a pre-treatment for apples and pears. I have a device that peels, coarsely cuts and quickly cuts apples and I recommend buying one if you plan to produce a lot of apples.

Melons, including cantaloupe, honeydew and watermelon, can be successfully dehydrated, but due to their high water content, they must be cut into thick slices (½ "slices) to leave something worth saving. They don't require preventive treatment.

Stone fruits, including cherries, plums, peaches, apricots and nectarines, must be washed and pitted. Smaller fruits, such as cherries and apricots, can be halved and placed on racks, while larger fruits should be cut from ¼ "to ⅜". All stone fruits, with the exception of cherries, require preventive treatment. The sulphite solution works best, especially for lighter colored fruits; although a citric acid solution will work if that's all that's available.

Blueberries, grapes and blueberries are unique among the fruits, as they dehydrate better if they are blanched first. Wash and remove the stems, then put them on a thin grill and immerse them in boiling water until cracks are seen on the skin. Then put them on the drying racks. The grapes will dry out better if you cut them in half.

Citrus fruits, such as lemons, oranges and grapefruits, can be successfully dried. Lemons and limes can be washed, cut into ¼ "sections and then dehydrated with the peel or peel. Oranges, grapefruits and other citrus fruits should be peeled off before sectioning and drying the sections on the shelves. Citrus fruits will be fragile when completely dry

Conditioning

When your fruit is ready, it should be conditioned before final storage. Conditioning is a process that allows humidity levels to equalize between individual pieces of fruit. In practice, this is achieved by placing the fruit in an airtight container and letting it sit sealed for a day or two.

If you notice condensation, put all the fruit back into the dehydrator for a few hours and try again. Otherwise, after the conditioning period it is ready for long-term storage.

Storage

The gold standard for storing dehydrated fruit is to seal it under vacuum and put it in a freezer at 10 degrees or less.

Even though I have done it sometimes, it makes using fruit too uncomfortable. In my opinion, it is exaggerated. One of the main advantages of dehydrated food is that electricity is not necessary for its conservation and the use of electricity to conserve it for ten years is somewhat exaggerated.

The vacuum seal is certainly worth it for the fruits that you do not intend to use soon. By evacuating the air, it removes atmospheric humidity and oxygen. Oxygen accelerates deterioration, so vacuum sealing improves the longevity of food. Vacuum bags are relatively expensive and are not always easy to reseal, so they are best used with items intended to be stored for a long time.

In my opinion, the best way to store dehydrated fruit is in wide-mouth jars. Although the cans admit light and air, which accelerates deterioration, as long as the cans are kept sealed and in a dark place when not in use, the negative effects are minimal. In addition, the cost savings that accumulate over the years of reuse combined with practicality make them perfect for the job.

Reconstituting Dried Fruit

Most dried fruits are consumed in this way due to their intense sweetness. However, there are cases where fruit rehydration will come in handy, such as crumbled apple added to oatmeal. In general, the fruits are adequately rehydrated if mixed with a volume of water approximately equal to the volume of nuts. Use water at room temperature, mix well with fruit and leave to rest for 30 to 45 minutes, stirring occasionally.

Although fruit and shots are dehydrated more frequently, vegetables should not be overlooked. In fact, most of the dehydrated products in my pantry are made up of various vegetables.

Even if I freeze many vegetables, especially when they will be used as a main dish, dehydration is much more convenient for the vegetables that will be used in soups and stews.

Just as most of the weight of the human body comes from water, most of the weight of vegetables comes from water.

Dehydrated vegetables take up much less space than fresh, canned or frozen vegetables. Using them is very convenient: just shake a handful from a jar and put the lid back on.

Vegetables tend to lose vitamin C during dehydration and storage, but all the other vitamins and minerals they contain remain intact.

Although there are exceptions, due to damage to the cell walls due to the dehydration process, most of the dehydrated vegetables do not work as well as an independent vegetable course with dinner.

As a general claim, this assumes that you want a reconstituted vegetable to look a lot like fresh produce.

However, if that lack of similarity won't stop you from trying vegetables with a unique flavor and texture, you'll find that the reconstituted vegetables, though distinctly different, are still perfectly delicious, assuming you started with a good product in the first place. .

Another good use for dehydrated vegetables is as a nutritional booster. When my daughter was small, she loved spaghetti but hated vegetables. So, I would like to sprinkle the dehydrated vegetables in the blender and add them to the spaghetti sauce during cooking.

However, where the dehydrated vegetables really shine is in soups, stews, sauces and condiments. Reading the packages of various seasoning mixes for steak and salads; you will find onion, garlic, chilli, carrots, parsley, lettuce and celery, among other ingredients. Vegetables in themselves provide important flavors for seasoning sauces and condiments. For soups and casseroles, they will absorb water as they simmer and since their cell walls have been damaged during dehydration, they will release their unique flavors to soups and casseroles more easily than even fresh vegetables.

Selecting Vegetables for Dehydrating

While it may seem unlikely when looking at some vegetables, such as broccoli, any vegetable can be dehydrated with excellent results as long as the appropriate procedures are followed. As with fruit, although most experts say that you should only use the best vegetables, my experience is that as long as a vegetable is basically healthy (i.e. not rotten), it can be improved by dehydrating it.

A courgette with an ugly stain that cannot be sold whole as fresh produce can still be dehydrated after the ugly stain has been removed. Celery or carrots that have started to limp in the refrigerator can be blanched and dehydrated with excellent results. While part of my supply of dehydrated vegetables comes from items brought from the vegetable garden and processed directly, most come from small lots made of items that would have ruined in the refrigerator.

"Only fresh vegetables in excellent condition can produce quality in the dry product. Withered ones should not be used; the deterioration has already begun in them. A moldy bean can give a whole lot a bad taste.
"If possible, pick vegetables early in the morning; prepare them and start the drying process as soon as possible."
If you have a dehydrator, a manufacture or a commercial unit, the vegetables can be dried overnight and extracted in the morning when more vegetables can be processed. This is an added benefit when using a dehydrator.
"If you dry with another method, the vegetables harvested at night must be carefully selected, cleaned and stored in the refrigerator. In the morning, prepare and dry.
"When immature beans (green or yellow) and young peas are dried, the results can be very satisfactory in appearance, taste and palatability. But too often they undergo an enzymatic change that loses flavor and develops an unpleasant hay smell. These vegetables, a once dried, they absorb moisture very quickly and this accelerates the change; but it can occur when the product is stored in tightly closed containers. Use fresh, tender and grown beans; use fully developed peas, but collect them before the pods turn yellow. ".

Vegetables must be thoroughly washed, the top and roots removed, then cut into roughly "thick" slices. They must have uniform thickness so that dehydration is uniform.

Preparing Vegetables

Proper preparation of vegetables is the key to effective dehydration and the key technique is bleaching. The cellular structure of vegetables is much tougher than that of fruits. Bleaching helps soften the walls so that moisture can be removed more easily from the cells. It also deactivates enzymes that otherwise predispose to deterioration. With the exception of onions and garlic, all vegetables benefit from bleaching.
There are two common forms of bleaching: immersion in boiling water and steam. Both are equally effective. I tend to prefer steam bleaching because you lose less

nutrients by dissolving in water and it is easier to clean because I have a steamer. On the downside, steam bleaching takes twice as long. The vegetables to be dehydrated must be blanched in boiling water for two minutes or blanched with steam for four minutes.

Most vegetables, with the exception of onion, garlic and tomatoes, must be blanched before drying, steamed or blanched.

Bleaching reduces the amount of decomposition microorganisms in the product, blocks destructive chemical changes, preserves or establishes color, checks the ripening processes by stopping the action of the enzyme and coagulates some of the soluble components, thus saving the content of vitamins. Relax the walls of the fabrics so that moisture can escape easily. It also helps delay unwanted changes in taste during storage and ensures satisfactory product reconstitution.

When blanched the vegetables to freeze them, they go straight from the pot into ice water before being sealed and frozen. But when you bleach the vegetables to dehydrate them, they go directly from the pot to the drying racks of your dehydrator.

The other important element of preparation is the size. Vegetables should be cut into small, uniform pieces before bleaching so that they can be effectively dehydrated. Vegetables that can be cut should not be cut more than ¼ "thick. Vegetables such as broccoli should be cut into pieces of no more than an inch.

Steaming food helps preserve nutrients.
The steam method is preferred because it does not remove nutrients during the bleaching process. This is the procedure to follow:

1. Select a pan with a snug lid.

2. Buy or make a grill to hold vegetables on boiling water. (We found an adjustable vaporizer in a local hardware store that does an excellent job.) Water shouldn't touch the product. Put about ½ "of water in the pan; the water should boil quickly before putting the prepared vegetables in the pan.

3. When placing the vegetables, the slices must be separated so that the steam can reach all the slices. Vegetables should not be stacked more than 2–2 ½ inches. The depth will depend on the capacity of the pan used.

4. Details on the amount of time each vegetable should be steamed, as well as other information, are shown on the next page in the form of a table.

After bleaching, the vegetables should be distributed on the shelves to dehydrate. They must be positioned in such a way as to allow adequate air circulation. Therefore objects such as potatoes, carrots etc. They must be positioned with a layer of depth. However, objects such as parsley or chopped cabbage can be stacked a little more and still have adequate air circulation.
In the dehydrator several varieties of vegetables can be placed simultaneously, placing a different variety on each shelf and the stronger smelling vegetables on the upper shelves. Again, don't mix fruits and vegetables.

Vegetable Pretreatment

Unlike fruits subject to discoloration and browning, most vegetables are more stable, so there is no need to pretreat after bleaching. There are some exceptions. Although it does not affect their quality, onions, sausages, parsnips, potatoes and some pumpkins tend to brown. If this is desired, it will be sufficient to pre-treat with citric acid or sulphite solution as described in the chapter on fruit.

Dehydrating

Dehydration is obtained by organizing prepared and pretreated vegetables on drying trays in a single layer without touching the edges. This will ensure complete drying.

Once the vegetables are placed, place the trays in the dehydrator and turn it on, setting the temperature between 120 and 135 degrees Fahrenheit. You do not want to use temperatures above 135 ° C or the vegetables may "harden". This means that the vegetable has developed a hard outer rind to prevent moisture from escaping from its inner layers; so it's better on the underside of that temperature range.

The time required depends on the amount of humidity in the product, the temperature, the humidity and other factors. As with fruit, it's not the end of the world if they spend too much time in the dehydrator, but too dry vegetables take longer to rehydrate. Without hardening, the vegetables should be left in the dehydrator until they become crunchy or crunchy. Because they are so dry, they don't require conditioning like fruits.

Specific Vegetables

While the above information on dehydrating vegetables provides a good overview, some vegetables have specific requirements for best success.

Beets should be cooked through and the skin removed. Then cut ⅛ "often and dehydrate.

Broccoli and cauliflower should be cut as they would have served, with the stems cut in half or a quarter before steam bleaching.

Brussels sprouts should be cut in half, blanched and placed face down in the dehydrator.

Cabbage should be stripped of the outer sheets and cut into ⅛ "thick slices, such as sauerkraut, before blanching and dehydration.

Artichokes require special treatment to obtain a good product. Cut the thick cores of the corazones and boil them in a standard solution of pretreatment with citric acid for six minutes before putting them in the dehydrator.

Okra, parsley, mushrooms and horseradish must not be blanched or pretreated.

Onions and garlic do not require pretreatment or bleaching and will be soggy when completely dry. Its spiciness is transferred to other foods, so don't dry them with other items.

Pretreatment of an onion helps prevent darkening, but it is not strictly necessary. Potatoes work best if they are completely cooked. Peel, cut them into ⅜ "slices and boil for 20 minutes (in unsalted water) before dehydrating. If you want a less time-consuming method, just bake in the oven, put them in the refrigerator overnight, then cut and Dehydrate them the next day, dry them until crispy, the dehydrated potatoes in this way can be pulverized in a good blender and used to prepare instant mashed potatoes.

Tomatoes, ripe or green, do not require pretreatment or bleaching. Some people like to remove the skin, and if you want to do it simply dip them whole in boiling water in a basket until cracks start to form, and then dip them in ice water. Then the skin slips easily. Personally, I don't remove my skin. Just cut into small or even slices, even wedges and dehydrate on the border between chewy and crunchy. Tomato powder dried in a good blender simplifies the reconstitution of tomatoes in tomato paste, or as a thickener in sauces or as a base for tomato soup.

Many people recommend storing dried tomatoes in olive oil. I specifically recommend AGAINST this practice, because botulism spores can survive dehydration and covering dried tomatoes in oil will exclude oxygen, creating a perfect environment for botulism toxin development.

Commercial operations that produce oil-dried tomatoes implement very rigid acidification protocols to ensure a pH high enough to inhibit botulism. This is not practical in a home kitchen.

Preservation of Dehydrated Vegetables

When the vegetables are completely dry, remove the trays from the dehydrator and loosen the vegetables from the net. When the net is completely free, the vegetables should be fresh enough to be placed in storage containers. Otherwise, let them cool a little more. However, do not let the dehydrated vegetables stay on the shelves for a long time, as they will begin to absorb moisture and will need to be dehydrated again.

Dehydrated vegetables must be stored in such a way as to exclude air so that the humidity in the air is not reabsorbed and must be kept away from light so that their colors do not bleach. I keep my vegetables dehydrated in jars with an airtight seal and in my pantry, away from light.

If you plan to store vegetables for a long time, the use of a vacuum sealer to exclude all oxygen and fully protect the product will increase its duration by at least double. If you want to take it to the next level, you can store the dehydrated vegetables vacuum packed in a freezer. Under these conditions, they will be usable longer than human life.

You can rehydrate the vegetables by adding boiling water and letting the mixture stabilize. The first thing that most beginners underestimate is the amount of water required. With the exception of vegetables, which rehydrate with one cup of water per cup of dried vegetables, all other vegetables require between 2 and 1/2 and 3 cups of water for a cup of dehydrated vegetables.

The second thing that beginners underestimate is the time it takes for vegetables to reabsorb water. Although some vegetables like spinach, okra and sweet potatoes rehydrate in about half an hour, most others will take between an hour and ninety minutes. Once boiling water is added, stir, cover and go do something else.

Since dehydration in a favorable climate does not require modern technology, dried meats and fish in various forms have been the backbone of diets in many traditional cultures for centuries. This is not surprising, as protein is essential for survival and an ounce of dried meat contains up to 15 grams of protein.

Dried meat and fish, generally called "jerky", are the places where you get the most out of your dehydrating money. The reason is because most commercial beef shots are full of chemicals and sugars, and if you can find a tear without chemicals, you'll have to sell it to your eldest son to pay for it. Meat and fish drying will provide you with an excellent amount of shots for snacks and instant soups, stews and broths on the go.

The real shot is obtained by finely cutting all the muscle meat and drying the strips in a dehydrator or in the sun where the weather is right. Sliced meat can be marinated, smoked or rubbed with spices to absorb flavors.

Much of what is called "jerky" in the supermarket is not made with whole muscle meat; it is made with cheap minced meat.

One reason for this is the cost, but another is that dried ground beef is easier to chew. One of the disadvantages is that, for safety reasons, beef jerks made from minced meat must be impregnated with nitrite. In my opinion, the jury has not yet decided on the safety of nitrite1, so this chapter deals with the production of dried meat with whole meat instead of minced meat.

Selecting Meat for Jerky

Almost all commercial beef in the United States is made from beef, but in theory almost all meats can be used to make jerky beef.

Other meats present greater risks of parasites and microbes, but these risks can be eliminated with adequate preparation and processing. A secondary problem with meats other than beef is that some meats, especially poultry, are not appetizing if they are not cooked in some way before being dehydrated.

In general, you want fresh, muscular meat that you would normally eat. If you don't usually eat ostriches or rabbits or if you don't like these meats, turning them into shots won't make you more appetizing.

The meats can come from the grocery store, from the courtyard cattle, from game and other places. You should be very aware of the faecal contamination potential of the surface of any meat. This is practically true of birds because of the way they are processed, but it can also happen with deer that have been gutted or something overlooked.

Pests also present risks. The Trichinella parasite is common in pig products, as well as bears and raccoons.
Recently, it has been reported in ground squirrels. Triquinella can be removed by freezing meat in portions no thicker than 6 "at a temperature below 5 degrees Fahrenheit for thirty days. Your typical freezer (like the one connected to your refrigerator) can't do it, but a good freezer can.
Check the temperature in the freezer with a thermometer and lower it if necessary.

Hunted meat can have a large variety of pests and diseases. The trills are quite common and are the larvae of a bot fly. These remain just below the surface of the skin and do not infect the flesh, so if the skin is peeled it is not a problem.
Tularemia can be a problem with rabbits and hares.

Commercially sold rabbits are tested. If you are hunting rabbits, wear gloves and a mask while peeling and if the liver has white or yellow spots, do not eat the rabbit! Tularemia is dangerous enough to be considered a biological warfare agent. The biggest concern for the largest hunted herbivores, such as deer and elk in the Rocky Mountains, is chronic frictional disease (CWD). CWD is a prion-based disease similar to "mad cow" disease and if a human being is infected it can take years to manifest. When it does, the resulting brain damage causes death. Until now, transmission to humans has only been demonstrated in a test tube. But since similar prion diseases in sheep and cows can be transmitted to humans and it can take decades to show signs in a human being, caution is needed. If you are a hunter, check with your state's game department to see if you are hunting in an area affected by the disease. If so, have the meat tested for CWD and do not use if positive.

Bovine spongiform encephalopathy (BSE), also known as "mad cow disease" is a more commonly known disease caused by prions. The prions that cause CWD, BSE and other spongiform encephalopathies are not, in their own terms, "live". They are aberrant proteins which, once introduced into the brain, cause other brain proteins to bend to imitate them. Viruses, parasites and bacteria can be destroyed with sufficient cooking, but prions cannot be destroyed by any amount of heat below full incineration. That's why you shouldn't be eating meat that has tested positive for CWD.

Prepare Meat for Jerky

Once the meat has been selected and processed for safety, it must be rinsed under running water and dried with paper towels.

The meat will cut more easily if you put it in the freezer for fifteen minutes first. Cut any visible grease and then cut into $1/8$ "and ¼" thick strips. Any length is fine. With red meat, it is generally easy to see the grain of the meat and, if cut perpendicularly to the grain, the squabble will be easier to bite and chew. Although it will work with any sharp knife, you will get the best results with a ceramic knife and a plastic cutting board. Personally, I use a nice, slightly sharpened carbon steel blade.

Theoretically, you can dehydrate the meat without seasoning or using the marinade, and I recommend it for the shots that will be pulverized later to create "instant broth". But in most cases, we recommend using a marinade because it will allow you to dehydrate at a temperature high enough to kill surface microbes without hardening the meat. Hardening of the carcass occurs when the outside dries so quickly that the moisture inside the meat cannot escape. Marinating meat first avoids this.

Marinades

Jerky marinades have some points in common with marinades for other purposes, but the nature of the jerky means that it should not contain added oils. In particular, vegetable oils should not come into contact with shots. Minerals such as iron will act as a catalyst to make vegetable oils rancid. To keep them at room temperature, manufacturers refine vegetable oils to remove minerals. If you add vegetable oil to a marinade for the jerk, minerals inside the meat, such as iron, will act as a catalyst, so the vegetable oil will develop bad flavors over time and the jerk's lifespan will drop dramatically.

Besides that, there are some basic concepts that can be worked out with infinite variations. Common to almost all marinated marinades are soy sauce and liquid smoke. There are many varieties of soy sauce available, but if you are sensitive to gluten you should make sure you choose a gluten-free variety. The salt in the soy sauce helps the meat stay longer (as long as it's sealed for storage) and doesn't provide enough sodium to be a medical problem for most people.

Soy sauce contains hydrolyzed soy protein. Although some soy sauces are a real fermented product, most use an industrial process. The soybean is ground and boiled in a hydrochloric acid solution, then neutralized with bleach. This process converts proteins into free-form amino acids and neutralizes the results in salt. That's why even the soy sauce without added salt contains a certain amount. The glutamic acid that is formed during hydrolysis gives a salty taste and the salt also improves the taste. Gluten-free soy sauce is perfect if you follow a caveman diet that excludes legumes because hydrolysis breaks down problematic proteins.

Liquid smoke is produced through what is called "destructive distillation of wood". It is literally smoke from a wood fire that has condensed into a liquid and bottled. If you've ever loaded into a container, the smoke that comes out of the container is what would be used to produce liquid smoke after the ash and solid waste are removed. Each time the wood is burned, a wide range of substances are produced, including potentially carcinogenic polycyclic aromatic hydrocarbons. But as we well know from traditional barbecue, smoked hams and bacon, smoked meat is quite tasty. In the quantities used for jerky production, liquid smoke remains well below the acceptable limits of use for carcinogenic compounds.
In addition to these two ingredients, marinades typically include ingredients such as onion powder, garlic powder, Worcestershire sauce and small amounts of cayenne pepper.

But you don't have to limit yourself to this! The meats should be left to rest in the marinade for twenty minutes to six hours in the refrigerator.

Basic Poultry Marinade
- ½ c. Soy sauce
- 2 tablespoons of Worcestershire sauce.
- 1 teaspoon onion powder 1 tsp. Garlic powder
- 1 teaspoon of liquid smoke
- ½ teaspoon black pepper
- ½ c. Sugar, honey or maple syrup (optional)

Ginger Poultry Marinade
- ½ c. Soy sauce
- 1 teaspoon apple cider vinegar
- 1 teaspoon of garlic powder ½ teaspoon. Ground ginger
- ¼ teaspoon black pepper

Fish Based Marinade
- ½ c. Soy sauce
- 1 teaspoon of liquid smoke
- 2 spoons of lemon juice
- ¼ teaspoon black pepper
- 2 tablespoons of maple syrup or molasses

Teriyaki Fish Marinade
- ½ c. Teriyaki sauce
- ¼ c. water
- ¼ c. Sugar or Honey (optional)
- 2 teaspoons of salt
- 1 teaspoon ginger powder
- 1 teaspoon garlic powder
- 1 teaspoon dried tarragon

Basic Pork Marinade
- ½ c. Soy sauce
- 1 tablespoon of Worcestershire sauce
- 3 teaspoons of liquid smoke
- 1 teaspoon apple cider vinegar
- 2 tablespoons of brown sugar
- Spoonful of ground cayenne pepper

Marinating Beef Teriyaki

- ½ c. Soy sauce
- ½ c. Worcestershire sauce
- ½ c. Teriyaki sauce
- 2 teaspoons of liquid smoke
- 1 tablespoon of brown sugar
- 2 teaspoons of garlic powder
- 2 teaspoons of onion powder
- ¼ teaspoon ground cayenne pepper

Meat Marinade

- ½ c. Soy sauce
- ½ c. Worcestershire sauce
- 1 tbsp honey
- 1 teaspoon black pepper
- 1 teaspoon onion powder
- 1 teaspoon of liquid smoke

Arrange the marinated strips of meat prepared on the trays of the dryer in a single layer without touching the edges. This will ensure complete drying. Once the strips are arranged, place the trays in the dehydrator and turn it on, setting the temperature between 145 and 165 degrees Fahrenheit. If you have not marinated the meat, keep the low end of the temperature range; But in any case, use temperatures not lower than 145 degrees Fahrenheit because it is important that meat reaches temperatures that kill pathogens.

Beef jerky marinades tend to have a very strong aroma and affect the taste of anything else dry at the same time, so jerky should be the only element in the dehydrator.

The time required for jerky preparation depends on the amount of humidity initially present in the meat, on the drying temperature, on the ambient humidity and other factors. The meat should be left in the dehydrator until it is difficult to fold (but it can still be folded) and you will see several cracks when you fold it.

Conditioning

Like the fruit, the idiot has enough residual moisture that must be conditioned before final storage. Conditioning is a process that allows humidity levels to equalize between individual shots. You can do this by placing the shots in an airtight container and letting it rest while it is sealed for a day or two.

If you notice condensation, put everything back in the dehydrator for a few hours and try again. Meat generally contains some fats that could be volatilized during dehydration, so check if the condensation you find is water or fat. If it is greasy (as evidenced by scrolling between your fingers), don't worry. If not, put it back in the dehydrator for a while, then repeat the conditioning process. After the conditioning period, your shots are ready for long-term storage.

Storage

The safest method of jerking is to seal it under vacuum and then put it in a freezer at 10 degrees or less. Dried meat stored in this way will remain throughout its life, but in my opinion it is an exaggeration.

Vacuum sealing is definitely good for gasps that you don't intend to use soon. By evacuating the air, it removes atmospheric humidity and oxygen. Oxygen accelerates deterioration; therefore, the vacuum seal improves the longevity of the food. Vacuum bags are relatively expensive and are not always easy to reseal, so they are best used with items intended to be stored for a long time.

In my opinion, the best way to store jerky for use in the coming months is in wide-mouth storage jars.

Although the cans admit light and air, which accelerates deterioration, as long as the cans are kept sealed and in a dark place when not in use, the negative effects are minimal.

DEHYDRATING BREAD

If you've ever used a mix of prepackaging, breadcrumbs or croutons, you've used dehydrated bread. These items are quite expensive and often contain ingredients (such as oils to attack spices) that you would prefer not to have. Dehydrating bread is fairly simple, but you can also go beyond simple bread by dehydrating cakes, pita bread and other baked goods.

Selecting Bread for Dehydrating

Although any bread can be dehydrated, the resulting product will be better maintained if the percentage of oils (especially vegetable oils) is minimal. This is because vegetable oils are very sensitive to the development of strange flavors and odors when mixed with anything else and left for a while at room temperature. If you are using commercial loaves of bread, read the label and make sure that the fat content is less than 2 g. Per serving.

It's even better if you can make your own bread using a bread yeast because when you make your own bread, you can check the ingredients. When preparing bread intended for dehydration with a bread yeast, if you replace the butter with coconut oil or palm kernel oil, the preservation qualities of the final product will be significantly improved thanks to the stability of these oils.

Another advantage of using a bread yeast is that you can incorporate spices (such as sage and rosemary to fill poultry) directly into the bread. This way, you can avoid relying on added oils to stick spices to dry bread. If you have a bread yeast, you already have dozens of recipes in the manual. If you want more information on how to bake bread, both with bread machines and with traditional natural leavening methods, you will find a lot of information in my book, The mini guide to agricultural fermentation.

The cake can also be dehydrated, but just as oils make a difference with the longevity of bread, they also make a difference with the cake. For this reason, it is best to make cakes to dehydrate. The only commercial cake that I have found suitable for dehydration is the angel cake.

For both recipes, use the bread yeast setting for 1 ½ pounds. loaf of white bread, with the "light" crust.

- 1 C. Water (heated to 80 degrees)
- 2 tablespoons of palm seed oil.
- 2 spoons of sugar
- 1 teaspoon and a half of salt
- 2 teaspoons of Bell Bird dressing
- 1-½ teaspoon bread yeast.
- 3 c. White bread flour

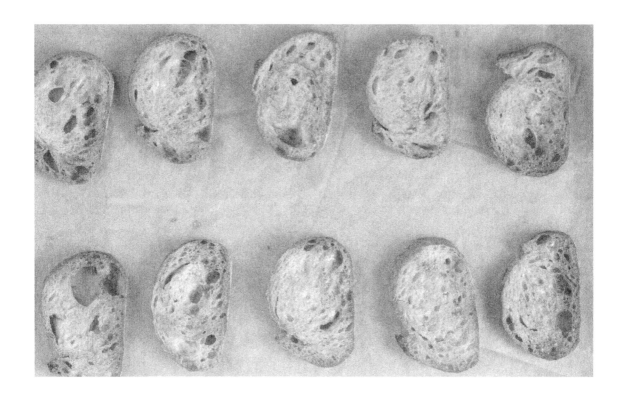

- 1 C. + 2 Water (heated to 80 degrees) Tbsp.
- 2 tablespoons of palm kernel oil
- 3 spoons of sugars
- 1 teaspoon and a half of salt
- 2 teaspoons of Italian dry seasoning
- 1-¼ teaspoon baking yeast
- 3 ¼ white bread flour

Cake Recipes

The key to preparing recipes that resist well after dehydration is the removal of oils that will become rancid. This includes egg yolk, butter and unstable polyunsaturated oils which would quickly spoil them. You still need a binder, so egg whites or an egg white product like Egg BeatersTM should be used.

After baking and cooling, the cake should be cut into ½ "cubes like croutons before dehydrating. The reason is because this allows you to reconstitute the cake more successfully. To reconstitute the dehydrated cake, place a cup of cake cubes in a ziplock plastic bag or bowl, sprinkle two tablespoons of hot water and mix thoroughly. Continue adding water gradually and stir gently until the cake reaches a cake-like consistency. This will take ½ to one cup of water, depending on the particular cake The taste of the reconstituted cake is better when heated, so you can heat it in the oven or with a short microwave excursion.

Mock Angel Food cake

- 2 C. All-purpose flour
- 2-½ baking powder (Rumford or another teaspoon without aluminum)
- ¼ teaspoon salt
- 1-½ c. sugar
- 2 teaspoons of vanilla extract
- 1 teaspoon of almond extract
- ¾ c. Egg whites
- ¾ c. Skimmed milk

The real angel cake reaches the yeast by beating the egg whites to incorporate the air, and then gently fold the flour.

It is a real delicacy if done well! Putting the real angel cake in a dehydrator would be a shame. So I developed a cake with a similar flavor (the secret is the 2: 1 ratio between vanilla and almond) which hopefully will not offend culinary sensitivity! Preheat the oven to 350 degrees. Use palm kernel oil or coconut oil to lightly grease a standard 13 x 9 cake pan.

Thoroughly combine the dry ingredients in one bowl and the wet ingredients in another, then carefully combine the wet and dry ingredients. Put the mixture in the pan and put it in the oven. It will take 30-40 minutes to finish. Starting at 30 minutes, try a toothpick in the center every five minutes until it's ready (when it comes out clean).

Leave the cake to cool on a wire rack, then cut it into ½ "cubes. Dehydrate at 135-145 degrees until crisp and hard.

Egg-Free Chocolate Cake

- ¾ c. All-purpose flour
- ⅛ c. Cocoa powder
- 2 teaspoons of baking powder
- ¼ teaspoon salt
- 1 teaspoon vanilla extract
- ⅓ c. sugar

Unsweetened Applesauce: enough to make a thick batter, about 1 to 1 ½ c.
This recipe is for a small chocolate cake that you can prepare in a small cake tin.
Grease the can with coconut or palm seed oil.
Preheat the oven to 350.

Mix the dry ingredients well. Then add the apple sauce, stirring constantly until you get the right consistency for the cake dough. Then add the vanilla extract and mix well. Put in the can and cook for 25-35 minutes.
After 25 minutes, try a toothpick in the center. If you don't (as indicated by the toothpick coming out clean), continue cooking in five minute increments until it's ready.
Cool the cake on a baking sheet then cut it into ½ "cubes and dehydrate at 135 degrees until crispy.

Preservation of dehydrated breads and cakes Dehydrated breads and cakes are fragile and easily turn into crumbs if not carefully packed and preserved.
Unlike other dehydrated products, they tend not to shrink too much during drying, so they can also be quite bulky. As with most dehydrated products, wide mouth mason jars work well, although we recommend using a quart size. Another approach is to use vacuum bags, capture as much air as possible and seal them without evacuating the air.
This will turn the bags into protective balloons. If the air is evacuated, external pressure would pulverize the bread or cake.

In the northeastern United States, most exotic spices, such as cinnamon, nutmeg and cloves, cannot be grown without a prohibitive artificial environment. But a large number of herbs commonly used for flavoring or infusions grow easily.

This includes ticks, basil, oregano, tarragon, rosemary, chamomile, anise, borage, cumin, dill, thyme, coriander, fennel, wild celery, sage and savory, among others. If you are interested in growing your own culinary herbs, I have a chapter dedicated to this topic in my book The Mini Farming Guide to Vegetable Gardening. It is very easy to do!

On my mini farm, I have two beds dedicated to growing herbs. I do it because some herbs, such as lemon verbena, are better used fresh, but also because growing and dehydrating my herbs for culinary use and tea saves a lot of money. In my local supermarket, only a couple of ounces of dried basil or tarragon cost a fortune. Since I enjoy using many herbs in my meals, growing and drying my herbs increases my profits. In addition, the quality of the herbs that you grow and dry out is usually higher. But even more valuable is the fact that I can grow herbs like salt and lemon balm that are not available in the supermarket.

The most important rule for this is the same as the most important rule for what you would grow in a garden or which vegetables you would dehydrate - just grow and dehydrate the herbs you really like. It makes sense to experiment a little with things you've never tried before, in case you like it. But if you don't like basil, dehydrating it is a waste of time.

In general, you want to harvest herbs during their most vigorous growth and before they establish the seeds to make them sweeter. You will also get more flavors if you collect them early in the morning before the sun evaporates the essential oils they have accumulated overnight.

Preparing Herbs for Dehydrating

Herbs must be washed well before drying due to the myriad of flying birds and running rodents. Once collected, the herbs should be washed thoroughly in cold running water and then gently dried in a salad spinner. The use of cold water helps to preserve essential oils. Rotating salads are available for $ 15 or less in major department stores.

Use a sharp pair of scissors to cut the desired part of the stem grass. Usually they will be sheets, although in the case of some herbs, such as chamomile, they will be flowers.

Just cut the desired part of the stem plant, but don't cut more sheets or flowers.

Dehydrating Herbs

The active ingredients of herbs are generally, but not always, essential oils that can be easily expelled from excess heat.

Even with herbs whose taste is primary due to non-volatile components, excess heat will often make them bitter. Therefore, herbs should be dried at temperatures no higher than 115 degrees Fahrenheit. Put the herbs on a fine mesh screen in the dehydrator and leave it until it becomes crispy.

Although the bottles of herbs that you will find in the supermarket are usually finely chopped or ground, this is the last thing you want to do with a herb until it is used. For conservation purposes, herbs should be kept as intact as possible.

The reason is because cutting or grinding dry grass exposes much more surface, which will simultaneously allow more flavoring compounds to escape, while reducing the flavor of the remaining oxidative components. Therefore, the desired portions of the herbs should be kept intact and practical.

Herbs are best chopped, ground or powdered immediately before use. If you've ever compared recently ground pepper from a pepper mill to one in a can at the grocery store, you'll see a huge difference. The same difference applies to any herb or spice.

Being delicate, dried herbs should be stored in a rigid container to protect them. Vacuum sealing is not practical because it would turn dry herbs into powder. You also want to store herbs so that there is as little space for oxygen as possible. Therefore, I recommend using the smallest cans available, which are generally 8 ounce or ½ pint cans. The sunlight creates havoc in the herbs, so keep them away from the sun.

Heat can cause unwanted changes in taste, as well as the loss of aromatic components, so keep them even in a cool place.

Modern lifestyles don't leave people with a lot of time, especially during the work week. In practice, this translates into a large number of foods consumed in restaurants, fast food and take-away dishes. Dehydration allows you to spend time when you have it on a weekend and take advantage of it by saving time during the week.

There are many ways to do this. My family cooks once a week, where various dishes are prepared on the weekend, stored in the freezer and then microwave for lunch and dinner throughout the week. Over time, we create a single dish, such as baked stuffed peppers and shepherd's pie, and we also store individual dishes and side dishes that can be mixed and combined.

Dehydrated foods can also help in general, since all the harvesting and cutting work has already been done. If you are preparing a saucepan and you need carrots, you don't have to remove a cutting board and a knife. (And you don't need to wash them.) Instead, pour a cup of dried carrots into the stew.

But dehydrated food can go much further, in the realm of almost instant food. If you've ever tried a cup of ramen or some instant packaged soup, you've probably noticed that the ingredients are dehydrated. You will also find that instant mixes of salad dressings, instantly flavored oatmeal and many other ready meals are little more than pre-cooked dehydrated ingredients.

Instant Food Principles

Foods intended for immediate use are precooked whenever they generally need to be cooked for consumption. For example, if you want to include broccoli, peas and carrots in an instant meal, they will be pre-cooked before dehydrating rather than blanching them. Apples don't have to be pre-cooked because apples are usually eaten raw, even if you wanted to prepare an instant apple sauce, you would cook them a little before dehydrating them.

The other principle is that of fine division. That is, everything you expect to rehydrate quickly will have to be as small as possible. Pre-cooked potatoes for use as instant mashed potatoes would be pulverized in a blender after dehydration to rehydrate more quickly. If you plan on making an instant apple-flavored oatmeal mix, the included apple pieces should be small.

The final principle is that of premixing. As for the bread filling recipe, in which the spices are cooked in the product, the dry ingredients of the instant food are combined and then packaged. Since the ingredients are dry and sealed, they do not mix until water is added and the resulting practicality saves time.

Instant Mashed Potatoes

Peel the potatoes, cut them into ¼ "slices and boil until they are tender. Using a perforated spoon to drain excess water, dry the potato slices in the dehydrator. Dry at 135 degrees until it becomes hard. Put the slices in a blender and pulverize them in a fine powder like that of the blender. Store in portions suitable for your family in vacuum bags until use.

To reconstitute, combine two cups of wet ingredient (boiling in a pan) for every 1 ⅓ cups of dry ingredient. The reason I vaguely specified it is because many people love milk in their mashed potatoes, while others are lactose intolerant.

Many people love butter in their mashed potatoes, but some people follow a diet that limits it. Its two cups of wet ingredients can be made up of any combination of water, milk, butter or other fats. Therefore, you can use 1 cup of water and 1 cup of skim milk if you are on a fat-free diet, or you can use 1 of cups of water and half a piece of butter (which equals a quarter cup) if you are intolerant. Since the batches vary slightly, the amount of liquid needed varies. Start with the umpteenth part of the liquid, then add a little at a time until you reach the desired consistency. Many people find that the flavor improves by adding up to half a teaspoon. salt for two cups of liquid ingredients.

The same technique used here can also be used with sweet potatoes, sweet potatoes, turnips, winter squash and any other vegetables generally served in a puree.

Bouillon

The bouillon is used as a base for soups and broths. Most of the broth you can find in the shop is mainly composed of salt or monosodium glutamate (MSG) with only a hint of true flavor. You can prepare your beef jerky broth, and it's considerably better.

The jerky used to prepare the broth should be marinated for a few hours before dehydrating using one of the basic recipes for marinating in the meat and fish chapter. He is then dehydrated for another twelve hours after which it would normally be considered done. This will make it difficult as a rock. Now, pulverize it in a high quality food processor. A rounded teaspoon of this powder will make a cup of broth or broth.

For an even better broth, sprinkle a little dehydrated celery, onion and sweet pepper. Mix this with the jerky powder in a ratio of ⅓ vegetable to ⅔ jerky.

The broth produced in this way must be well sealed so that it does not go wrong when removing moisture from the air. But as long as you keep it sealed when not in use, it will last for years.

Vegetable soup needs an aromatic base combined with some solid ingredients. The aromatic base is composed of onion powder and celery powder in a 2: 1 ratio and the solid ingredients are made up of small pieces of dehydrated vegetables such as tomato, pepper and carrot. Salt is commonly present as a flavor enhancer.

Instant Vegetable Soup

- 1 teaspoon Onion powder
- ½ teaspoon celery powder
- ½ teaspoon salt
- 1 dehydrated pepper, coarsely chopped spoons.
- 1 dried carrot, coarsely chopped spoon
- 1 teaspoon of dehydrated tomato, coarsely chopped Store in an airtight package until use.

This recipe can be multiplied as many times as you want. Add a cup of boiling water to 3 tablespoons of instant vegetable soup. Stir and let stand five minutes before enjoying.

Instant Tomato Paste

If you've ever tried making homemade canned spaghetti sauce, chances are you're frustrated that you can't get it as thick as commercial sauces. Commercial sauces can be thickened without burning because excess water is removed by a vacuum process that cannot be easily duplicated on a household scale. Thickeners such as flour or cornstarch should not be used in canning because they can make a product that is not properly preserved. The solution is in the perfect thickener: dehydrated tomato powder.

Dehydrate the tomatoes as indicated in the chapter on the dehydration of vegetables, with the exception of drying until it becomes crunchy. Let them cool, then put them in a food processor and turn them into powder. Store the powder in an airtight container away from light and heat.

Instant tomato paste can be used to make tomato paste by mixing it gradually with hot water until the desired consistency is reached. If used as a thickener in sauces, it will absorb three times its volume of water.

You can also use it to prepare tomato soup, but if used for this purpose, mix with onion powder and celery powder in a ratio between 5 parts of tomato and 2 parts of onion and 1 part of celery by volume. To prepare the tomato soup, add a cup of boiling water to ⅓ cup of this mixture, stir and leave to stand covered for five minutes.

Instant Oatmeal

The individual packets of instant oatmeal in the grocery store are ridiculously expensive compared to the retail cost of their raw ingredients. You can save a lot of money by buying the large round packets of instant oatmeal and then adding your ingredients to create single-serving bags using zippered sandwich bags.
Looking at the ingredients and nutritional label of a popular "oatmeal and cinnamon" instant oatmeal variety, it becomes clear that one third of the weight of the product is sugar, cinnamon and dehydrated apples provide a negligible amount and the budget is oatmeal.

To create your superior product, combine the following for a single serving:

- ⅓ c. Instant oatmeal
- ⅓ c. Dried fruit
- 1 tablespoon of sugar (less if desired)
- Any spice you want

Dried fruit should be divided into small pieces, no larger than any ¼ "size for easy rehydration. To use, put the mixture in a bowl and add between one and a cup of boiling water. Stir and let stand covered for a few minutes.

Instant Salad Dressings

I eat a lot of salad, but I don't like premade salad dressings because many contain non-food ingredients.

Examples of non-food ingredients I've seen on salad dressing labels include propylene glycol (safe antifreeze), disodium inosinate, disodium guanylate, FD&C Blue 1 Aluminum Lake, etc.

Dry blends are a little better, but since their most dominant ingredients are sugar, salt and MSG, they are not worth the cost. It is much better to create your own. The main advantage of grocery store blends is that they contain guar gum, xanthan gum and similar ingredients that help mix oil and vinegar. But if you don't mind shaking the bandage before pouring it, you have not lost anything and have gained a lot by doing yours.

Instant Italian Seasoning Mix

- 1 tbsp sugar
- 1 tablespoon of salt
- 1 teaspoon garlic powder
- 1 tablespoon of onion powder
- ¼ teaspoon celery seeds
- ½ teaspoon of dehydrated hot pepper, well broken
- 1 tablespoon of dried oregano
- 1 tablespoon of dried parsley
- 1 teaspoon dried basil
- ½ teaspoon of black pepper flakes
- ½ teaspoon of thyme

The recipe above does a little more than enough for three lots, so feel free to multiply as needed. Store in an airtight container in a cool place away from sunlight. To turn it into an Italian seasoning, mix two tablespoons with ⅔ cup of olive oil, ¼ cup of vinegar and two tablespoons of water.

Shake vigorously, then shake immediately before use.

RECIPES

HERBS AND SPICES

Basic Garlic Powder

Here is the basic method of preparing your garlic powder. Below is a variation, my opinion on my mother's roast beef dressing. I give the mix a rougher tone with the addition of one of the basic foods of my kitchen: smoked paprika. In addition to using it on roast beef, you can also try it on roasted chicken or add it to sauteed onion when you season chickpeas as a side dish. You could also use it in baked tofu for your next quick vegetarian meal.

MAKES 2/3 CUP [75 G]
- 4 cloves of garlic, peeled and cut into thin slices
- 1 teaspoon of fine sea salt

1. Cover the dehydrating trays with non-stick netting sheets lightly coated with cooking oil.

2. Place the garlic slices on the prepared trays. Dry at 125 ° F [52 ° C] for 15-20 hours, until the garlic slices are completely dry and break once folded. Let it cool completely.

3. In a spice grinder, working in batches, pulverize the garlic into a very fine powder, adding about 1/2 teaspoon of salt to each batch to prevent sticking. (To avoid clogging the mill, start grinding with the mill upside down and then turn it upside down.)

4. Store in an airtight container, preferably with a pack of silica gel to prolong freshness, in a dark place at room temperature for up to 6 months.

Roasted Meat Seasoning, Smoked

Mix 2 tablespoons of basic garlic powder, 2 teaspoons of smoked paprika, 4 tablespoons of kosher salt and 2 teaspoons of freshly ground black pepper. Store in an airtight container, preferably with a silica gel pack to prolong freshness, in a dark place at room temperature for up to 6 months.

MAKE 1/2 CUP [60 G]

Turmeric-Ginger-Lime Powder

A turmeric tonic is one of those home remedies that can make me feel alive when my head is full of congestion or sore throat. I use this powder in the drink recipe below, where turmeric tastes quite delicious in an intensely golden way, especially if you use a generous hand with honey. You can also add this ocher yellow powder to your next curry to get an explosion of turmeric flavor that is far more delicious than you can get from a store-bought spice jar.

MAKES ABOUT 1/3 CUP [20 G]
- 1 lime
- 85 g of fresh turmeric root, peeled and cut into thin slices
- 60 g of fresh ginger root, peeled and cut into thin slices

1. Cover the dehydrating trays with non-stick netting sheets lightly coated with cooking oil.

2. Using a potato peeler, remove only the bright green zest from the lime peel. (Reserve the rest of the file for another use, including, if desired, a spritz in the finished infusion.)

3. Place the strips of lime zest and the slices of turmeric and ginger in a single layer on the prepared trays. Dry at 135 ° F [57 ° C] for 6-8 hours, until the turmeric and ginger slices are completely dry. Let it cool completely.

4. In a spice grinder, sprinkle the lime zest, turmeric and ginger in a fine powder.

5. Store in an airtight container, preferably with a silica gel pack to prolong freshness, in a dark place at room temperature for up to 6 months.

Turmeric -Ginger-Lime Zinger

When I went to Bali, I was regularly offered a turmeric, ginger, lime and honey drink, and here I recreated the drink in an easy-to-prepare mix. Put 3/4 teaspoon of turmeric, ginger and lime powder in a cup. Add 1 cup [120 ml] of boiling water and stir to dissolve. Add 1 teaspoon of honey or more to taste. Light with a little fresh lime juice, if you wish, before serving. For an extra dose of breast cleansing power, mix the slightest pinch of cayenne pepper into your drink.

MAKE 1 BEVERAGE

Kimchi Powder

Kimchi, a fermented Korean spicy cabbage that is often used as a seasoning, is surprisingly versatile when dried. These days, you can buy fresh, prepared kimchi in most supermarkets with specialty stalls, such as Whole Foods. After drying the kimchi, you can leave it in its leaf state, ready to add flavor, warmth and a little chewy texture to your backpacker meals. For home use, I dry the kimchi and then turn it into a powder, which I use as a flavor enhancer filled with umami for pasta soups, rice porridge, mashed potatoes and even quesadillas. I especially love the supercharging of Dijon mustard with kimchi powder. It's like combining the strengths of all the best hot dog ingredients: sauerkraut, mustard, chili pepper and seasoning. Kimchi's styles vary greatly in the texture and warmth of the chili, so choose a kimchi that tastes good in the refrigerated state before drying.

MAKES ABOUT 1/4 CUP [40 G]
  -   1 cup [210 g] of prepared kimchi, drained

1. Cover the dehydrating trays with non-stick netting sheets lightly coated with cooking oil.

106

2. Place the kimchi on a thin layer on the prepared trays. Dry at 135 ° F [57 ° C] for 12-18 hours, until the kimchi is fragile and completely dry to the touch. Let it cool completely.

3. In a spice grinder, working in batches, spray the dried kimchi powder.

4. Store in an airtight container, preferably with a pack of silica gel to prolong freshness, in a dark place at room temperature for up to 2 months or in the freezer for up to 1 year.

Kimchi Mustard

Mix 2 tablespoons of Kimchi powder in 1/2 cup [120 ml] of high quality Dijon mustard (I like Fallot). Transfer to an airtight jar and let it rest in the refrigerator so that the flavors mix for at least 1 day. Stir to mix. Store in the refrigerator for up to 6 months.

MAKE 1/2 CUP [85 G]

The following recipes are for 1 ½ pounds bread. Put the water on the bottom of the pan, add the mixed dry ingredients (except the yeast) to the bread pan, evenly distribute the fats in the four corners of the pan, then place the yeast in the center of the dry ingredients. The water should be heated to about 90 degrees before adding it to the pan. Follow the instructions on the bread yeast to make 1 ½ lbs. bread with a slightly golden crust.

Apricot Nut Bread

Yield: 1 loaf of bread
- 1 cup of diced dried apricots
- 1 cup of milk water
- 2 ½ cups of all-purpose flour
- 3 teaspoons of double-acting yeast
- ½ teaspoon salt
- 2 eggs, lightly beaten
- ¾ cup of sugar
- 2 tablespoons of butter, melted
- ½ cup of chopped walnuts

1. Immerse the apricots in water until they are reconstituted.

2. Grease a 9 × 5 × 3 inch bread pan and carefully cover with wax paper.

3. Sift the flour, baking powder and salt.

4. Gradually beat the eggs and sugar.

5. Drain the liquid from the apricots, add enough milk to the liquid to equal 1 cup, then put the liquid in a 3-litre bowl.

6. Mix the egg, butter and drained apricot mixture, then add the flour and nut mixture and beat well.

7. Pour into the prepared pan. Leave to stand for 10 minutes, then cover with another pan of the same size and put in the oven at 350 ° F. Bake for 20 minutes, then uncover and bake for another 50 minutes or until the bread tests are ready.

8. Remove from the pan to cool the grill before cutting.

Banana Bread

Yield: 1 large loaf or 2 small loaves
- 2 cups of dehydrated bananas
- 2 cups of hot water
- 2 ½ cups of sifted flour
- 1 cup of sugar
- 3 and a half teaspoons of baking powder
- 1 teaspoon salt
- 3 spoons of vegetable oil
- ¾ cup of milk
- 1 egg
- 1 cup of walnuts, finely chopped

1. Immerse the bananas in hot water until reconstitution, then drain.

2. Beat the flour, sugar, baking powder, salt, vegetable oil, milk, egg and reconstituted bananas.

3. Mix well; beat at medium speed for half a minute, constantly scraping the side and bottom of the bowl. When well mixed, add the walnuts.

4. Pour into a 9 × 5 × 3 inches floured and greased bread pan or into two 8 ½ × 4 ½ × 2 ½ inch trays.

5. Bake at 350 ° F 55–65 minutes or until the wooden tip inserted in the centre is clean.

6. Remove from the pan; cool well before cutting.

Yield: about 42
- ¾ cup of dehydrated bananas
- 1 cup of water
- 5 cups of all-purpose flour
- 3 teaspoons of baking powder
- 1 teaspoon of baking soda
- 2 teaspoons of salt
- 1 teaspoon nutmeg
- ¼ cup of butter
- 1 cup of sugar
- 1 ½ teaspoon vanilla
- 3 well-beaten eggs
- ½ cup of buttermilk

1. Soak the bananas in water for half an hour.

2. Sift flour, baking powder, baking soda, salt and nutmeg.

3. Beat the butter, then mix and beat until the sugar, vanilla and beaten eggs are soft. Beat the mixture well for 2 minutes.

4. Stir and mix the drained reconstituted bananas and the buttermilk well.

5. Add the flour mixture in 3 or 4 portions, stirring enough to mix after each addition. Cool the dough before rolling it.

6. Remove a quarter of the dough from the refrigerator at a time, knead slightly 4-5 times, spread it on a thick, floured cloth and cut with a 2½ "floured doughnut.

7. Fry in deep fat heated to 350 ° F until golden brown, then lift and drain on paper towels. If desired, the dough can be well covered and stored in the refrigerator for 1 or 2 days, for frying if necessary.

Banana Muffin

Yield: 8–10 rolls
- 1 cup of dehydrated bananas
- 1 cup of water
- 1 cup and a half of all-purpose flour
- 1 ¼ teaspoon of baking powder
- ½ teaspoon of baking soda
- 1 teaspoon salt
- 3 spoons of sugar
- 2 small eggs
- ¼ teaspoon grated lemon zest
- 1 teaspoon lemon juice
- 3 tablespoons of buttermilk
- 3 spoons of butter

1. Preheat the oven to 400 ° F and grease 8–10 cups of the medium muffin tray.

2. Immerse the plane trees in water until they are reconstituted.

3. Sift flour, baking powder, baking soda, salt and sugar.

4. Beat the eggs, then add the reconstituted bananas. If mixed, add lemon zest, lemon juice, buttermilk and butter. Mix well

5. Add the liquid mixture all at once to the dry ingredients; Stir quickly and vigorously until the flour is moistened, but no more.

6. Place the dough on the prepared trays and put them in the preheated oven.

7. Cook for about 30 minutes or until golden brown. Serve hot.

Banana Waffles

Yield: 7-inch waffles
- 1 cup of dehydrated bananas
- 1 cup of water
- 2 cups of all-purpose flour
- 3 teaspoons of baking powder
- 1 tbsp sugar
- ¾ teaspoon of salt
- 3 eggs
- 1 ½ cups of milk
- ⅓ cup of melted butter

1. Immerse the bananas in water until reconstitution, then drain.

2. Sift the flour, baking powder, sugar and salt.

3. Beat the eggs, then add the milk and melted butter. If mixed, pour into dry ingredients.

4. Add the reconstituted bananas and beat the mixture until smooth.

5. Using 1/2 cup of dough for each waffle, cook on a hot waffle until it turns golden brown.

6. Serve immediately with butter, hot syrup, icing sugar or fruit puree.

Corn Pancakes

Yield: about twenty 4-inch pancakes
- ¾ cup of cornmeal
- 1 cup of boiling water
- 1 cup of buttermilk
- 2 eggs
- 1 cup of whole wheat or white flour
- 1 tablespoon of baking powder
- 1 teaspoon salt
- ¼ cup of cooking oil

1. Grind a cup of dehydrated corn in a grain mill. This will be equivalent to ¾ cup of cornmeal.

2. Mix all the ingredients well, then cook on a hot plate.
Note: Cornmeal pancakes will take longer to bake, as cornmeal will take longer to bake flour.

Cornbread

- 1 cup of whole wheat or white flour
- ¼ cup of white or brown sugar
- 4 teaspoons of baking powder
- ¾ teaspoon of salt
- 1 cup of cornmeal
- 1 cup of milk or buttermilk
- ¼ cup of liquid butter
- 1 egg yolk
- 2 egg whites
- A plate of cornbread is perfect for any meal.

1. Grind 1 ⅓cups of dehydrated corn in a grain mill. This will produce 1 cup of cornmeal.

2. Mix flour, sugar, baking powder, salt and cornmeal.

3. Add milk or buttermilk, liquid butter and egg yolk. Beat the mixture until smooth.

4. Beat the egg whites until stiff, then fold the dough.

5. Pour into an 8 × 8 × 2 inches greased pan and bake in a preheated oven at 425 ° F for 20–25 minutes.

Crunchy Fried Corn Cakes

- Yield: 8 cakes
- 1 cup and a half of cornflour
- ¾ teaspoon of salt
- 1 ½ cups of boiling water
- ⅓ cup of butter

1. Grind 2 cups of dehydrated corn in a grain mill. This will produce 1 ½ cups of cornmeal.

2. Put the cornmeal and salt in a bowl and slowly add boiling water, stirring the mixture as you make until you get a smooth and stiff enough dough to shape it.

3. Carefully shape the dough into flat oval cakes.

4. Heat the butter in a 10-inch pan until the butter sizzles but does not smoke. Place the cakes and fry them quickly, until each side has a vibrant golden colour; about 3-4 minutes. Do not rotate the crayons until this intense colour develops. Serve with butter

Prune Nut Bread

Yield: 1 loaf of bread
- 1 cup of prunes or prunes
- ½ cup of orange juice
- ½ cup of hot water
- ½ teaspoon of grated orange zest
- 2 cups of all-purpose flour
- 3 teaspoons of baking powder
- ½ teaspoon salt
- ½ teaspoon of cinnamon
- ¾ cup of sugar
- 1 tablespoon of butter, melted
- 2 beaten eggs
- ½ cup of chopped walnuts

1. Grease an 8 × 4 × 2 ½ inch pan.

2. Chop the prunes into small pieces, then pour the orange juice, hot water and grated orange zest over them. Leave the mixture to rest for 10 minutes, then add the melted butter and beaten eggs.

3. Sift flour, baking powder, salt, cinnamon and sugar, then add to the plum mixture. Mix well

4. When the wet and dry ingredients have mixed, add the chopped walnuts.

5. Pour into the prepared pan and bake at 350 ° F for 1 hour or until bread tests are performed. Remove from the mould to the mould to cool.

Crispy Apple Cake

- 2 cups of dehydrated apples
- 2 cups of water
- 1 cup of oatmeal
- 1 cup of flour
- ½ cup of brown sugar
- ½ teaspoon of baking soda
- ½ cup of margarine or butter (1 stick)

1. Immerse the apples in water until reconstitution, then drain.

2. Mix oats, flour, brown sugar, baking soda and margarine (or butter) until they crumble.

3. Stroke half the mixture on the bottom of an 8 × 8-inch pan. Spread the apples over the crumbly mixture. Sprinkle with sugar and cinnamon and cover with the remaining crumbs.

4. Bake at 350 ° F for 1 hour. Serve hot or cold with a scoop of ice cream.

Note: Apples can replace reconstituted dried peaches, apricots or prunes.

- 2 cups of dehydrated apples
- 2 cups of water
- ½ cup of sugar
- 1 cup of lightly compacted light brown sugar
- 1 teaspoon cinnamon
- 1 spice mix

1. Immerse the apples in water until they are reconstituted, then cook them until they are completely tender; drain and reserve liquid.

2. Add the sugar. Stir until the sugar dissolves, then mash the apples and add enough reserved liquid until the mixture has the consistency of apple sauce.

3. Combine the apple sauce with brown sugar and cinnamon.

4. Spread evenly on the bottom of an oiled 13 × 9 × 2 inch oblong pan.

5. Mix according to the directions on the spice mix.

6. Carefully pour the dough over the apple sauce layer. Bake about 35 minutes at 350 ° F.

7. Remove from the serving dish and pour the apple sauce mixture evenly from the bottom of the pan over the cake. Serve hot, topped with whipped cream or ice cream.

Cherry Coffee

Yield: 10-15 portions
- 3 cups of dehydrated cherries
- 3 cups of water

Follow the recipe for apple coffee cake, except for the drained reconstituted cherries instead of the apples and sprinkle 1 cup of sugar evenly over the fruit.

Peach Coffee Cake

Yield: 10-15 portions
- 3 cups of dehydrated peaches
- 3 cups of water

Follow the recipe for apple coffee cake, except use empty reconstituted peaches instead of apples and sprinkle ¾ 1 cup of sugar evenly on the fruit.

Rhubarb Cake

- 1 cup of dehydrated rhubarb
- 2 cups of hot water
- ½ cup of butter
- 1 ½ cups of brown sugar
- 1 beaten egg
- 1 cup of buttermilk
- 2 cups of sifted flour
- 1 teaspoon of baking soda
- ½ cup of white sugar
- 1 teaspoon cinnamon

1. Immerse rhubarb in water until reconstitution, then cook covered until almost tender. When it is almost tender, drain it.

2. Beat the butter and brown sugar, then add the beaten egg. Add the buttermilk, flour and baking soda alternately.

3. Lightly fold the discharged rhubarb into the batter, then roll out the batter into a greased and floured pan.

4. Sprinkle the top with sugar and cinnamon and bake at 350 ° F for 30–35 minutes.

Simple Vanilla Cake

- 2 C. All-purpose flour yeast (Rumford or other 2 tsp non-aluminum powder)
- 1 teaspoon of baking soda
- ¼ teaspoon salt
- 1 C. sugar
- 1 C. Sugar-free apple sauce
- 1 teaspoon vanilla extract
- ¾ c. Egg whites
- ¾ c. Skimmed milk

Preheat the oven to 350 degrees. Use palm kernel oil or coconut oil to lightly grease a standard 13 x 9 cake pan.

Carefully combine the dry ingredients in one bowl and the wet ingredients in another. Once the oven is preheated, combine the dry and wet ingredients, then pour the mixture into the pan and put it in the oven. It will take 30-40 minutes to finish. Starting at 30 minutes, try a toothpick in the center every five minutes until its ready (when it comes out clean).

Leave the cake to cool on a wire rack, and then cut it into ½ "cubes. Dehydrate at 135-145 degrees until crisp and hard.

Chocolate Cake

- 3 c All-purpose flour
- 2 C. Cocoa powder
- 3 teaspoons of baking soda
- 2 teaspoons of salt
- 1 C. Egg whites or Egg BeatersTM
- 2 tablespoons of vanilla extract.
- 2 C. sugar
- 1 C. Sour cream without fat or without fat / without sugar 3 c. Yogurt
- Unsweetened Applesauce

This recipe is for a fairly large batch of cake, so you can cut the proportions in half if necessary. It has been designed for use with two 13 x 9 glass trays. As with bread recipes, it is important that the dry ingredients for this recipe are measured correctly. Use a set of dry measuring spoons. Put the dry ingredient in the bowl until it overflows. DO NOT pack.

DO NOT pour the ingredient directly into the cup. This will cause compaction and lose proportions.
After the dry measurement overflows, use the straight back of a kitchen knife to remove the excess.

This recipe will stick to trays with a vengeance. To avoid this, grease the pan with coconut oil or palm oil, insert a piece of cut wax paper to fit it in the pan, then lightly grease the wax paper before adding the ingredients.

Preheat the oven to 350. Stir the dry and wet ingredients separately, then mix the dry and wet ingredients just enough to make sure everything is well moistened and incorporated. Pour into molds and cook for 30-40 minutes. After 30 minutes, try a toothpick in the center. If you don't (as indicated by the toothpick coming out clean), continue cooking in five minute increments until it's ready.
Cool the cake on a baking sheet, then cut it into ½ "cubes and dehydrate at 135 degrees until crispy.

Dried black olives in the dehydrator acquire a new consistency and flavor; crunchy like potato chips but rich in its dark wine flavor. Use it as a finishing touch on vegetables, grilled fish or your next tuna casserole.

MAKES ABOUT 1 CUP [100 G]
- 2 cups [400 g] of chopped and chopped Kalamata olives
- 2 teaspoons of finely grated lemon zest

1. Cover the dehydrating trays with non-stick netting sheets lightly coated with cooking oil.

2. In a medium bowl, mix the olives with the lemon zest to combine. Distribute the mixture on the prepared trays. Dry at 135 ° F [57 ° C] for 10 to 14 hours, until the olives are dry and crunchy. Let it cool completely.

3. Chop the olive mixture again.

4. Store in an airtight container, preferably with a silica gel pack to prolong freshness, in a dark place at room temperature for up to 3 months.

Persian cuisine uses the brilliant combination of rose and cardamom in many desserts; it is a delicate and evocative way to make something as simple as a shortbread biscuit linger on the palate. I love these cookies with afternoon tea or broken into pieces dusted with vanilla ice cream.

MAKES 32 BAR
- 2 cups |240 g| of all-purpose flour
- 11/3 cups |120 g| of oatmeal
- 1 teaspoon salt
- 3/4 teaspoon ground cardamom
- 11/3 cups |290 g| of unsalted butter, at room temperature
- 150 g caster sugar |150 g|
- 2 tablespoons of pink sugar
- 1 teaspoon rose water

1. Preheat the oven to 135 ° C [275 ° F]. Butter a 23 x 33 cm pan and cover the bottom with parchment paper.

2. In a large bowl, mix flour, oatmeal, salt and cardamom for all uses. Set aside.

3. Combine the butter, granulated sugar and rose sugar in the bowl of an electric mixer equipped with the attachment of the scoop (or in a medium bowl with a manual mixer). Beat at medium speed until creamy and light light, about 2 minutes. Mix in the rose water. With the mixer on low speed, gradually add the flour mixture, 1 cup [115 g] at a time, and beat only until combined.

4. Press the dough into the prepared pan; A clean glass works well for pushing the mixture into the corners and smoothing the surface. Using a butter knife or a counter knife, cut the dough lengthwise to form eight uniform strips. Cut the dough transversely to form four equal strips, for a total of thirty-two bars. Prick the surface of the dough with the teeth of a fork.
5. Cook until golden brown, but not golden brown, 80 to 90 minutes. Remove the pan on a wire rack and allow to cool for about 15 minutes.

6. Turn the pan upside down to release the pastry on a cutting board and remove the parchment. Carefully divide the biscuit into bars along the cutting lines (it is also possible to cut the hot bars again with a sharp knife if the incisions have not been maintained during cooking). Let it cool completely.

7. Store in an airtight container at room temperature for up to 1 month.

There's nothing like the luminous intensity of this marigold-colored sugar to add interest to a sugar cookie or spice up your favorite muffin recipe. You can also use it as an easy way to add intrigue to your iced tea - mix it with the double-soaked hot tea before pouring it over ice. To combine the orange and lemon zest, I like to use a sharp Y-shaped peeler to remove only the brightly colored peel in strips, leaving the marrow white.

Since the citrus peel is easy to dry, I always do a little more than I need for sugar. Later, I will add a small strip of shell to a stew or soup; I am always amazed by the fragrance and the depth it imparts.

MAKES ABOUT 1¼ CUPS [115 G]
- Zest of 3 navel oranges
- Zest of 2 lemons
- 150 g of sugar [150 g]

1. Place the strips of orange and lemon zest on the trays of the dehydrator. (It is not necessary to align the trays, as the strips are large enough not to fall into the standard holes of the tray and are not sticky.) Dry at 135 ° F [57 ° C] for 8 to 12 hours, until dry and crispy. Let it cool completely.

2. Break the rind into small pieces. (You can do this easily by inserting the zest in a zip lock pouch and then touching and rotating it with a rolling pin.)

3. In a spice grinder, working in batches, sprinkle the zest with about two thirds of the sugar in a very fine powder with a few pieces of peel. (To avoid clogging the grinder, start grinding with the grinder upside down and then turn it clockwise.) Sift the powder from the grated sugar to remove any remaining grated particles. Add the remaining sugar.

4. Store in an airtight container, preferably with a silica gel pack to prolong freshness, in a dark place at room temperature for up to 6 months.

FRUIT

Agave-Kissed Sour Cherries

During the excursions, the dried black cherries make my family climb hills, rocks and waterways. At the farmers market, when I see fresh black cherries (or "cakes") during their short season, I jump to dehydrate them. If you dry them untreated, they are an excellent ingredient in casseroles, but they are not a snack material. In this recipe, I dry them first and then dip them in lightly sweetened syrup with agave syrup. I unload them and dry them again briefly, so they are ready to move on to the next batch of wholemeal salad, cookie dough with double chocolate chip or a takeaway bag to climb a mountain. If you cannot find fresh cherries, check if your supermarket can freeze the cherries without sugar. In this case, simply defrost them in the refrigerator and drain them before drying.

MAKES A 3/4 CUP [75 G]
- 9 pound fresh sour cherries [910 g], stem
- 1/2 cup [120 ml] of water
- 2 tablespoons of agave syrup
- 1 teaspoon of balsamic vinegar

1. Cover the dehydrating trays with non-stick netting sheets lightly coated with cooking oil.

2. Boning the cherries. Distribute them in a single layer on the prepared trays. Dry at 135 ° F [57 ° C] for 22-26 hours, until they are wrinkled and feel soft when pinched.

3. In a medium non-reactive saucepan over high heat, bring water, agave syrup and balsamic vinegar to a boil. Add the dried cherries, stir and lower the heat. Boil for 2-3 minutes. Remove from the heat and let the cherries rest in the syrup for about 20 minutes, then drain them.

4. In the meantime, wash and dry the dehydrator trays and cover them with net sheets lightly coated with cooking oil.

5. Place the cherries on prepared trays. Dry at 135 ° F [57 ° C] for 1 hour, until dry to the touch. Let it cool completely. You can choose to pack dried cherries at this point.

6. Store in an airtight container, preferably with a pack of silica gel to prolong freshness, in a dark place at room temperature for up to 1 month, in the refrigerator for up to 2 months or in the freezer for up to 1 years.

What I love about sandwiches is the way the crisp edges converge with the soft and tender interiors, something that can be difficult to find outside of a domestic kitchen. Sandwiches in cafes tend to be too large, shapeless and tasteless. These are simple scones with a little acidity from yoghurt to echo the bittersweet glory of dried sour cherries. For an extra citrus kick, sprinkle the rolls with more citrus sugar instead of Demerara sugar. Eat two if you are hungry; you will have even more corners to snack on. This is a small batch since the sandwiches are not designed to hold them long. Double the recipe if you have a crowd.

MAKES 8 SMALL SCONES
- 2 cups [240 g] of all-purpose flour
- 4 tablespoons [50 g] of citric sugar or granulated sugar
- 2 teaspoons of baking powder
- 1 teaspoon of baking soda
- 3/4 teaspoon salt
- 5 tablespoons [70 g] of cold butter, cut into 1/2 inch [12 mm] pieces
- 1/2 cup [50 g] dried black cherries kissed by agave (opposite page), cut into large pieces
- 80 ml of the whole yoghurt
- 1/3 cup [80 ml] of cream, plus 2 tbsp
- 2 eggs
- 2 teaspoons of grated orange zest (if using granulated sugar)
- 1 tablespoon of Demerara sugar or granulated sugar

1. Preheat the oven to 200 ° C [400 ° F]. Liner a baking sheet with parchment paper or a silicone baking sheet.

2. In a large bowl, mix flour, citrus sugar, baking powder, baking soda and salt. Add the pieces of butter to the flour mixture and mix to coat. With cold fingers, rub the butter into the flour mixture until the combination has a predominantly grainy consistency with a few pea-sized pieces of butter covered in flour. Add the dried cherries and mix to distribute evenly.
3. In a small bowl or liquid measuring spoon, mix the yoghurt and 1/3 cup [80 ml] of cream, one of the eggs and the orange zest (if used). Prepare a well in the flour

mixture and pour the cream mixture. Stir until combined to form a moist and sticky paste. Using lightly floured hands, roll the dough into a rough ball.

4. On a lightly floured work surface, whisk the dough into an approximately circular mass of about 15 cm wide and 4 cm thick. Using a bench scraper or a butter knife, cut the dough into eight even pieces (or six pieces, if you want a bigger sandwich). Place the wedges on the prepared pan, leaving about 5 cm between the sandwiches.

5. In the small bowl, mix the remaining egg with the 2 tbsp cream to wash the eggs. Brush the top of each sandwich evenly with the beaten egg. Sprinkle each sandwich with a little Demerara sugar.

6. Bake for 20-25 minutes, until the tops of the sandwiches, are golden brown. Serve hot or at room temperature.

Vermouth Dried Cherries

Manhattans are a delicious cocktail, but their cherries sometimes disappoint. In my first foray into creative dehydration (as part of an article I did for Slate), I had the idea of dipping cherry in vermouth, the key aromatic element of a Manhattan, and then drying it up to obtain a consistency pleasantly chewy. The remaining soaking liquid could enter the cocktail, pushing the cherry flavour forward. Mixed with whiskey, these elements add irresistible shades to the classic cocktail.

MAKES A 3/4 CUP [90 G]
- 680 g of fresh cherries, such as Bing or Lambert, derived
- 2 cups [480 ml] of red vermouth (like Martini and Rossi)

1. Boning the cherries. Add them to the vermouth in a pan. Soak for 8 hours or overnight, mixing once or twice.

2. Cover the trays of the dryer with non-stick mesh sheets lightly coated with cooking oil.

3. Drain the cherries (pour the soaking liquid into a sterilized jar and set aside to prepare the cocktails; it will remain for several months at room temperature). Distribute them on the prepared trays. Dry at 135 ° F [57 ° C] for 24 hours or until it is no longer soft, but pleasantly chewy. Let it cool completely. You can choose to pack dried cherries at this point.

4. Store in an airtight container, preferably with a pack of silica gel to prolong freshness, in a dark place at room temperature for up to 1 month, in the refrigerator for up to 2 months or in the freezer for up to 1 years.

Manhattan Dried Cherry

Here is a classic Manhattan rye in which the cherry flavour becomes little higher thanks to the infused cherry vermouth left behind by dipping the fruit. Since the drink is fruity, do not choose sweet bourbon like Maker's Mark for this drink, but stick to a more robust whiskey like 1776 or Bulleit rye.

Yield: 1
- Broken ice
- 60 ml of rye whiskey
- Cherry vermouth with 1 oz |30 ml|
- 2 dashes of bitters, Angostura for traditional flavour or bitter with Xocolatl mole aroma for a touch of spice
- 1 dried vermouth cherry

Fill a jug with crushed ice. Add rye, vermouth and bitters and stir to mix. Pour into a cold cocktail glass and garnish with the dried cherry. Serve immediately

Puree of Any Dried Fruit

Yield: 2 and half cups
- Excellent for baby food or older children who make fruit whips.
- 1 kilo of wet dried fruit
- 1 ½ cups of water
- ⅔ to 1 ⅓ cups of sugar depending on the acidity of the fruit

1. Wash the fruit quickly but thoroughly in cold water, removing it in a 3 litre saucepan. Add water, which should reach 1 inch above the top of the fruit. Cover and dip 1–3 hours—Cook in the same water in which the fruit was immersed. Now heat to a boil over moderate heat, then reduce the heat and simmer until tender, 15-20 minutes. Add the sugar in the last 5 minutes of cooking and cook until the sugar dissolves. Remove from the heat and cool to room temperature, then drain, saving juice.

2. Turn the fruit into a sieve or crusher and rub well to get all the puree. Alternatively, put the fruit in a bowl and use the kitchen scissors or a cookie cutter to finely cut the fruit (or use a commercial unit to blend). If the puree is thicker than desired, add enough drained juice to get the desired consistency. A frozen puree is preferred for cake fillings and a medium for whipping fruit.

3. To store, pour the puree into a sterilized jar with a tight lid and refrigerate.

Note: use the remaining juice on fruit cups or drinks.

Dried Apricot Puree

Yield: 2 cups

Excellent for making ice cream or fruit smoothies for serving babies or older children.
Stewed apricots as described in Stewed dried apricots. Add sugar or leave without sugar, depending on how the puree is used.
Convert the apricots into a sieve or crusher placed on a bowl. Leave to stand until the syrup is drained. Pour the syrup into a container and store it for fruit cocktail or for a drink.
Now rub the fruit through the sieve or the crusher to get all the puree. There should be 2 cups of starchy mashed potatoes. If you want a thinner puree, dilute with a little drained juice.

Stewed Dried Apples

Yield: 6 cups of thick sauce
- 1 kilo of dried apples
- ½ cup of sugar
- 5 cups of cold water

1. Put the apples in a 4-litre saucepan; add cold water, cover and soak 3-4 hours (although this may not be necessary). Heat to a boil over moderate heat, then reduce heat, cover and simmer for 15 to 20 minutes or until smooth, but not tender.

2. Add the sugar and simmer another 5 minutes. Remove it from the heat. Leave to cool lukewarm or cold.

Stewed Apricot Dried

- 1 pound of dried apricots
- 1 cup of sugar
- 6 cups of cold water
- Pinch of salt (optional)
- For attractive and appetizing results, use clean, brightly coloured fruit.

1. Wash quickly but thoroughly in cold water. Put the fruit in a 3-litre saucepan, add water, cover and let stand 1–2 hours. Then place on moderate heat until the fruit begins to boil vigorously. Immediately reduce the heat over low heat and cook for 12-15 minutes longer or until smooth.

2. Add sugar and salt and simmer another 5 minutes. Remove from heat to cool lukewarm or cool to serve alone or with cream.

Sweet and hot spices, such as fennel, cinnamon, cardamom and ginger, which infuse the tea for chai, can be used for other good uses, such as this gummy pineapple treatment. Store the sweet marinade in a jar in the refrigerator; It will also work with apples, pears and mangoes, and you can use it to sweeten iced tea or lemonade.

MAKES 2 CUPS [50 G]
- 2 cups |480 ml| of water
- 1 cup |200 g| of sugar
- 1/4 teaspoon fennel seeds
- 1 cinnamon stick
- 10 green cardamom pods
- Three 1/2 slices in |12 mm| thick peeled fresh ginger
- 1 pineapple, peeled, animated and cut into 2.5 cm pieces

1. In a medium saucepan over medium-high heat, combine water, sugar, fennel seeds, cinnamon stick, cardamom pods, ginger and cloves and bring to a boil. Turn off the heat and add the pineapple. Set aside and leave to rest until cool. Store in the refrigerator for at least 1 hour or overnight.

2. Cover the trays of the dryer with non-stick mesh sheets lightly coated with cooking oil.

3. Drain the pineapple, reserving the syrup for another use, if desired. Place the pineapple pieces on the prepared trays. Dry at 135 ° F [57 ° C] for 18-24 hours, until the pineapple is dry to the touch and chewy. Let it cool completely. You can choose to pack the pineapple at this point.

4. Store in an airtight container, preferably with a silica gel pack to prolong freshness, in a dark place at room temperature for up to 3 months or in the freezer for up to 1 year.

When you receive fresh fruit from a seller in a Mexican market, you will often have the opportunity to sprinkle it with chilli pepper, salt and some lime, small accents that highlight the juicy sweetness of a mango or melon. Drink it. I gave this idea another look at this combination of sweet and savoury dried fruit. Ancho pepper powder provides a light aromatic aroma, while an optional touch of cayenne pepper will give the mango a firmer bite.

MAKES 2 CUPS [45 G]
- 5 teaspoons of fresh lime juice, plus 1 lime, cut into slices of about 3 mm | 1/8 inch (optional)
- 2 teaspoons of agave syrup
- 1/4 teaspoon ground chilli pepper
- 1/4 teaspoon of fine sea salt
- Pinch of cayenne pepper (optional)
- 2 large ripe, peeled, pitted and sliced 3/8 inch | 1 cm] mangoes

1. Cover the dehydrating trays with non-stick netting sheets lightly coated with cooking oil.

2. In a large bowl, mix the lime juice, agave syrup, ancho pepper powder, sea salt and cayenne pepper (if used) together. Add the mango slices to the mixture and mix gently to coat evenly.

3. Place the mango slices and the lime slices (if used) on the prepared trays. Dry at 135 ° F [57 ° C] for 4-6 hours, until the handle is rubbery and dry to the touch and the files are crisp and break when folded. Let it cool completely.

4. In a spice grinder, working in batches, pulverize the dried lime slices into a very fine powder.
5. Store in airtight containers, preferably with silica gel packets to prolong freshness, in a dark place at room temperature for up to 3 months or in the freezer for up to 1 year.

Blueberries, although tasty, need a little help. They have hard skin and are too bitter to be appreciated when they dry themselves. Here, I cook them briefly to pop the skins and soak them in a sweetened orange juice. Then they dry in bittersweet and are perfect for cooking and devouring directly. (They are even less sweet than the sugary dried cranberries found in the grocery store.) As an additional by-product, the soaking liquid can be used to create a cute, alcohol-free pink spray with carbonated water or champagne.

MAKE ABOUT 1 PT [100 G]
- 3 cups [720 ml] of fresh orange juice
- 2 cups [400 g] of sugar
- 2 pt [400 g] blueberries, rinsed and collected

1. In a large non-reactive saucepan over medium-high heat, combine the orange juice and sugar. Stir until the sugar dissolves. Add the blueberries, bring to a boil, then lower the heat and simmer for a few minutes until you hear the blueberries burst. Stir for 1 to 2 minutes, until most of the blueberry peels have split. Leave to cool, then refrigerate the blueberries in the liquid overnight. Drain the blueberries, reserving the liquid if desired.

2. Cover the trays of the dryer with non-stick mesh sheets lightly coated with cooking oil.

3. Place the blueberries, separated from each other, on the prepared trays. Dry at 135 ° F [57 ° C] for 20-24 hours, until they are a little leathery on the outside and no longer soft in the center. Mix the blueberries and rotate the trays several times during the drying process, and be sure to separate any berries that have piled together. Let it cool completely. You can choose to pack blueberries at this point.

4. Store in an airtight container, preferably with a silica gel pack to prolong freshness, in a dark place at room temperature for up to 3 months or in the freezer for up to 1 year.

Dried Cinnamon Apples

This is the basic type of dry and chewy apple that I grew up with, but he gave me an apple pie with some sugar and cinnamon. While these are tasty to munch on their own, I really love them mixed with hot morning breakfasts and baked goods. They mix particularly well with fresh fruit in a cake or cobbler; dried apples will absorb some of the fresh fruit juice and help prevent a lumpy crust.

MAKES ABOUT 13/4 CUPS [35 G]
- 2 pounds [910 g] of sour apples (such as Granny Smith or Braeburn), peeled, cored and cut into 1/3 inch slices [8 mm]
- 2 tablespoons of fresh lemon juice
- 1 tbsp sugar
- 1/2 teaspoon cinnamon
- Pinch of salt

1. Cover the dehydrating trays with non-stick netting sheets lightly coated with cooking oil.

2. In a large bowl, combine the apple slices and lemon juice and mix to coat well. Sprinkle with sugar, cinnamon and salt and mix to coat well.

3. Place the apple slices on the prepared trays. Dry at 135 ° F [57 ° C] for 6-8 hours, until dry, elastic and still flexible. Turn the apples over and turn the trays at least once during the drying process. Let it cool completely. You can choose to pack the apples at this point.

4. Store in an airtight container, preferably with a silica gel pack to prolong freshness, in a dark place at room temperature for up to 3 months or in the freezer for up to 1 year.

These translucent orange slices are beautiful. In fact, I have seen similar slices tied together in garlands that create a nice decoration for a shop. A perfect cross section can serve as an exquisite cake topper, cheese plate or ice cream, but don't let the decorative charm keep you from eating it. The chips offer an intense citrus flavor with a surprising and clear consistency. They are also a perfect complement for mulled wine and cider. You can also use the fine cut method for mandarins, grapefruits and blood oranges, but since we are leaving the skins out, I think navel oranges offer the best combination of sweetness and bitter undertones. These orange slices will be crunchier in the first two weeks.

MAKES 4 CUPS [170 G]
- 4 navel oranges
- 2 teaspoons of olive oil
- 1/8 teaspoon of sea salt

1. Cover the dehydrating trays with non-stick netting sheets lightly coated with cooking oil.

2. Cut the very thin oranges transversely (1/8 in [3 mm] or less) and put them in a medium bowl. It is useful to use a serrated knife to cut these thin slices. Gently mix the orange slices with the olive oil and salt.

3. Place the orange slices in a single layer on the prepared trays. Dry at 135 ° F [57 ° C] for 12-18 hours, until it is very dry and cool. Let it cool completely.

4. Store in airtight containers, preferably with a silica gel pack to prolong freshness, in a dark place at room temperature for up to 2 months.

All the best drinks have a sour note, and this is definitely a cocktail-inspired dessert, sweet but with remarkable depth. Here, the dehydrator is used to speed up the final phase of a traditional candied peel recipe, drying the exterior that wraps around a dense and resistant citrus interior.

MAKES 4 CUPS [120 G]
- 3 grapefruit peels, cut into 1/2 in [12 mm] wide strips
- 3 cups [600 g] of sugar
- 3/4 teaspoon Angostura bitters or other bitters

1. Fill a medium non-reactive pot with water and bring to a boil. Add the grapefruit peel, cook for 30 seconds, then drain. Set the shells aside in a bowl. Fill the pot with fresh water and repeat the bleaching process two more times.

2. In the same pan over medium-high heat, combine 2 cups [480 ml] of water, 2 cups [400 g] of sugar and bitters and stir until the sugar dissolves. Add the grapefruit peel, medium heat and simmer for 40-50 minutes, until the peel is translucent, very soft and shiny. Remove from the heat and allow the shells to cool completely in the syrup.

3. Drain the grapefruit peels. Fill a small bowl with the remaining 1 cup [200 g] of sugar. Mix a few pieces of peel at a time in the sugar, covering them, then remove the extra sugar.

4. Cover the dehydrator trays with non-stick mesh sheets.

5. Place the pieces of the shell on the prepared trays. Dry at 135 ° F [57 ° C] for 11/2 hours, until dry to the touch but still moist inside. Let it cool completely.

6. Store in airtight containers, preferably with parchment paper between each layer of shells (to prevent sticking) and a pack of silica gel to extend freshness, in a dark place at room temperature for up to 1 month.

Dried Pineapple with Chai Spices

Sweet and hot spices, such as fennel, cinnamon, cardamom and ginger, which infuse tea for chai, can be used for other good uses, such as this pineapple gummy candy. Store the sweet marinade in a jar in the refrigerator; It will also work with apples, pears and mangoes and you can use it to sweeten iced tea or lemonade.

MAKES 2 CUPS [50 G]
- 2 cups [480 ml] of water
- 1 cup [200 g] of sugar
- 1/4 teaspoon fennel seeds
- 1 cinnamon stick
- 10 green cardamom pods
- Three 1/2 slices in [12 mm] thick peeled fresh ginger
- 10 teeth
- 1 pineapple, peeled, animated and cut into 2.5 cm pieces

1. In a medium saucepan over medium-high heat, combine water, sugar, fennel seeds, cinnamon stick, cardamom pods, ginger and cloves and bring to a boil. Turn off the heat and add the pineapple. Set aside and leave to rest until cool. Store in the refrigerator for at least 1 hour or overnight.

2. Cover the trays of the dryer with non-stick mesh sheets lightly coated with cooking oil.

3. Drain the pineapple, reserving the syrup for another use, if desired. Place the pineapple pieces on the prepared trays. Dry at 135 ° F [57 ° C] for 18-24 hours, until the pineapple is dry to the touch and chewy. Let it cool completely. You can choose to pack the pineapple right now (see page 21).

4. Store in an airtight container, preferably with a silica gel pack to prolong freshness, in a dark place at room temperature for up to 3 months or in the freezer for up to 1 year.

Sometimes my kids made fun of me while working on new recipes for this book. They don't want chilli on their dried mango or vermouth on their dried cherries; they like their simple and direct dry foods. This fruit skin recipe couldn't be simpler. Use the best of early summer (spicy apricots and raspberries) in a snack. Honey slightly softens the acidity and provides a slight note of floral complexity. Add the honey gradually and try to measure

MAKES 8 TO 10 PORTIONS
- 1 pt | 170 g | raspberries
- 680 g of apricots, halved and pitted
- 1/4 cup | 60 ml | of water
- 2-3 tablespoons of honey

1. Cover the dryer trays with non-stick leather fruit sheets.

2. Combine raspberries, apricots and water in a large food processor (or blender). Work in a smooth puree. Add 2 tablespoons of honey and mix well. Try to decide if the mash needs more sweetener; If so, add the remaining 1 tablespoon of honey.

3. Using a displaced spatula or the back of a spoon, distribute the puree on the prepared trays, making the edges a little thicker than the center. Dry at 135 ° F [57 ° C] for 4-6 hours, until the mixture is leathery and dry to the touch. (You can speed up the process by peeling the mixture off the non-stick sheet and turning it after about 3 hours, even if it isn't necessary.)

4. Peel the fruit skin off the non-stick sheet. Cut into individual portions and roll up in a plastic wrap or parchment paper. (If using parchment, tie or tie the roll to hold it together.)

5. Store in an airtight container, preferably with a silica gel pack to prolong freshness, in a dark place at room temperature for up to 2 weeks or in the refrigerator for up to 1 month.

Rhubarb isn't a fruit, it's a vegetable, but it's good enough for one, and this rather pale snack is just what it does at the end of winter, when rhubarb is the only seasonal item in your backyard and you're sitting waiting for spring to come. You can start your fruit leather practice before the relentless weather in summer, when everything ripens at once. Here, I used a small banana to provide a leather frame for rhubarb and it softens the acidity of rhubarb. This is a fruit skin where some sugar is needed, as rhubarb alone is very acidic. When preparing rhubarb, cut and discard the toxic green sheets on the stem and cook only the stem.

MAKES 8 TO 10 PORTIONS
- 680 g [1180 l] rhubarb, peeled, cut into 1/2 inch slices [12 mm]
- 1/2 cup [120 ml] of water
- 1/2 cup [100 g] of sugar
- 1 teaspoon vanilla extract or 1 vanilla bean
- 2 ripe bananas, peeled and cut into pieces

1. Cover the dryer trays with non-stick leather fruit sheets.

2. In a large non-reactive saucepan over medium heat, combine rhubarb, water and sugar. Add the vanilla and mix. (If you use a vanilla bean, cut it in half lengthwise and scrape the seeds in the pan.) Cook, stirring occasionally, until the rhubarb is tender, about 10 minutes.

3. Put the rhubarb mixture in a large blender with bananas. Blend until the mixture becomes a very soft golden pink puree. Using a displaced spatula or the back of a spoon, spread the puree on the prepared trays, making the edges a little thicker than the center. Dry at 135 ° F for 6-8 hours, until dry to the touch, rotating the trays at least once. (You can speed up the process by peeling the mixture off the non-stick sheet and turning it after about 3 hours, even if it isn't necessary.)
Put a spatula under the dough to loosen it and let it cool completely.
4. Peel the fruit skin off the non-stick sheet. Cut into individual portions and roll up in a plastic wrap or parchment paper. (If using parchment, tie or tie the roll to hold it together.)

5. Store in an airtight container, preferably with a silica gel pack to prolong freshness, in a dark place at room temperature for up to 2 weeks or in the refrigerator for up to 1 month.

VEGETABLES

Buttered or Creamed Green Beans

Yield: 4-5 portions
- 2 cups of dehydrated green beans
- 2 cups of water
- ½ teaspoon salt
- 1 teaspoon of sugar
- Melted butter or medium béchamel

1. Immerse the green beans in water until reconstitution, then cook over medium heat until tender.

2. Add salt, cook another 5 minutes, then drain the liquid. Add sugar and butter or medium béchamel and serve immediately.
Butter beans are an excellent side dish.

Green Beans in Egg Sauce

Yield: 4 portions
- 1 ½ cups of dry green bean
- 3 cups of water
- 2 spoons of margarine
- 2 tablespoons of flour
- ½ cup of milk
- ⅛ teaspoon of celery seeds
- ¼ teaspoon pinch of salt
- 3 sliced boiled eggs

1. Immerse the green beans in water until reconstitution, then cook over medium heat until tender. Drain, reserving ½ cup of liquid.

2. Melt the margarine in a saucepan and add the flour. Stir, then slowly add milk and reserved liquid.

3. Stir constantly; cook until the mixture boils and thickens, then add the celery salt, salt and pepper. Mix well. Gently fold the eggs.

4. Heat the sauce and pour over the hot beans placed on a preheated serving dish. Serve immediately

Green Beans and Sauce

Yield: 6 portions
- 2 cups of chopped green beans
- 4 cups of water
- ½ teaspoon salt
- 1 can of mushroom cream
- ½ cup of grated cheese

1. Boil the beans in water until tender, then add salt and simmer another 5 minutes. Drain, reserving ¼ cup of liquid.

2. Mix the mushroom cream with the reserved liquid.

3. Alternate the layers of drain and soup in a pan.

4. Sprinkle with cheese and bake at 350 ° F for 30 minutes.

Beets in Orange Sauce

Yield: 4 portions
- 1 ½ cups of dehydrated and grated red beets
- 1 ½ cups of water
- 3 spoons of sugar
- 2 tablespoons of corn starch
- ¼ teaspoon salt
- ½ cup of orange juice
- ¼ cup of lemon juice
- ⅛ teaspoon of orange peel
- ⅛ teaspoon lemon zest

1. Immerse the beets in water until reconstitution, then cover and cook over medium heat until tender. Drain.

2. Mix sugar, cornstarch, salt, lemon juice and orange juice in a double boiler. Cook on boiling water until thick and clear, stirring constantly.

3. When it thickens, add the lemon zest, orange peel and cooked and drained beets. Stir slightly. Cook on boiling water until completely cooked. Serve immediately.

Sliced Beets with Lemon Juice

Yield: 10-12 portions
- 3 cups of dehydrated sliced beetroot
- 6 cups plus 4 spoons of nutmeg water
- 1 cup of sugar
- 2 spoons of butter
- 2 tablespoons of whole cloves
- 4 cinnamon sticks
- 2-3 lemons, in the juice
- 2 tablespoons of corn starch

1. Simmer the beets in 6 cups of water until they are tender. Drain, reserving 2 cups of liquid.

2. Put cloves, cinnamon and nutmeg in a gauze bag and knot. Place the bag in the reserved liquid—Cook for 2 to 3 minutes. Add sugar, butter, lemon juice and drained beets—Cook for 2 minutes.

3. Remove the spice bag and pour the juice into another pan.

4. Add the cornstarch and 4 tablespoons of water to the juice. Mix well and cook for 2 minutes before pouring over the beets. Heat and serve.
Note: colour the mixture if necessary. The toppings should be tasted. The sauce tastes better if left to rest for about a day.

Yield: 4 portions
- 1 ½ cups of dehydrated red beets
- 1 ½ cups of water
- 2 tablespoons of butter or margarine
- 2 tablespoons of flour
- ¾ cup of milk
- 2 spoons of vinegar
- ½ teaspoon of sugar
- ¼ teaspoon salt
- a pinch of pepper

1. Immerse the beets in water until they are reconstituted, then cover and cook over medium heat until tender; drain.

2. Melt the butter or margarine in a saucepan and mix with the flour. If mixed, gradually add the milk. Stir until the mixture is smooth and thick, then add vinegar, sugar, salt and pepper.

3. Serve on drained hot beets.

Buttered Carrots

Yield: about 5 portions
- 1 cup of dehydrated carrots
- 2 cups of water
- ½ teaspoon salt
- 2 tablespoons of chopped dehydrated parsley butter
- Butter carrots are a tasty addition to any meal.

1. Immerse the carrots in water until reconstitution, then cook over medium heat until they are tender, for about 30 minutes. Add salt and simmer another 5 minutes.

2. Remove the lid to evaporate the remaining liquid, watching carefully to avoid burns. Add the butter and sprinkle with parsley.

Carrots in Orange Sauce

Yield: 4 portions
- ½ cup of dehydrated carrots
- 1 cup of water
- ⅓ teaspoon of salt
- 2 teaspoons of corn starch
- 1 tablespoon and a half of sugar
- ½ cup of orange juice
- 1 tablespoon or more of coconut milk
- 1 tbsp butter

1. Immerse the carrots in water until reconstitution, then cook over medium heat until tender.

2. Mix salt, cornstarch, sugar and orange juice until smooth and add to the carrots. Cook and stir until thick and light.

3. When thick, add coconut milk and butter. Heat to a boil. Serve hot.

Buttered or Creamed Peas

Yield: 5 portions
- 2 cups of dehydrated peas
- 4 cups of water
- ½ teaspoon salt
- 2-3 tablespoons of butter

1. Immerse the peas in water until reconstitution, then cook over medium heat until tender. Season with salt and cook another 5 minutes.

2. Empty the liquid if necessary; Pour the melted butter or a light béchamel sauce and serve immediately.

Note: equal quantities of reconstituted, drained and cooked peas, cauliflower or celery can be combined and spread with butter.

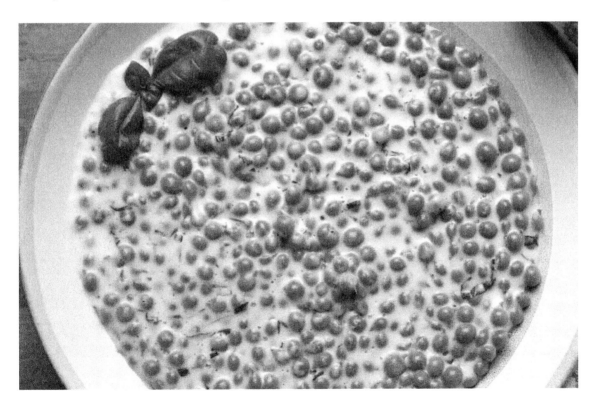

Creamed Peas and New Potatoes

Yield: 4 portions
- 2 cups of dehydrated potatoes
- ¾ cup of dehydrated peas
- 1 teaspoon dried onion
- 4 ¼ cups of water
- 2 tablespoons of dehydrated radishes
- 1 ¼ teaspoon salt
- ½ cup of evaporated milk
- 2 spoons of butter

1. Immerse the potatoes, peas and onions in 4 cups of water until reconstitution.

2. Cook the reconstituted potatoes, peas and onions until tender, about 30 minutes. Drain the liquid, reserving ½ cup.

3. Immerse the radishes in ¼ cup of water until reconstitution. Drain.

4. Add salt, evaporated milk, butter and liquid reserved for cooked vegetables. Boil slowly until the liquid thickens slightly. Add the drained radishes just before serving.

Sweet Potato and Cheese Casserole

Yield: 4 portions
- 4 cups of dehydrated sweet potatoes
- 4 cups of water
- 1 teaspoon salt
- 1 tbsp sugar
- 1 cup of milk
- ¾ cup of grated cheese
- 1 tbsp butter
- Salt and pepper to taste

1. Immerse the potatoes in water until they are reconstituted—Cook over medium heat, covered, until the potatoes are tender. Season with salt and cook another 5 minutes, then drain the liquid.

2. Pour into a 5-cup saucepan into 2 or 3 layers, sprinkling each layer with salt, pepper and sugar. Pour the milk over and sprinkle with cheese, then sprinkle with butter.

3. Bake uncovered for 15 minutes at 375 ° F.

Yield: 4 portions
- 4 cups of dehydrated spinach
- 4 cups of water
- 3 slices of bacon
- 3 tablespoons of flour
- 1 ½ cups of milk
- ¾ teaspoon of salt
- ¼ teaspoon pepper
- 1 cup of grated cheese
- 4 ounces of cooked pasta

1. Put the spinach and water in the saucepan and cover. Boil the spinach until tender, about 10 minutes, then drain.

2. Cut the bacon into small pieces and brown until golden brown, but not crispy. Remove the bacon from the fat and mix the flour and milk with the drops. Cook and stir until the mixture is smooth and thick.

3. When it thickens, add salt, pepper and drained spinach. Heat well.

4. Sprinkle the grated cheese on the cooked spaghetti and pour the spinach with hot cream; Sprinkle the pan-fried bacon and serve.

Zesty Instant Italian Dressing Mix

- 1 tbsp sugar
- 1 tablespoon of salt
- 1 teaspoon garlic powder
- 1 teaspoon onion powder
- ½ teaspoon dehydrated chilli, well broken
- 1 teaspoon dried oregano
- 1 teaspoon dried basil
- ½ teaspoon of black pepper flakes
- ¼ teaspoon cayenne pepper powder

The recipe above does a little more than enough for three lots, so feel free to multiply as needed. Store in an airtight container in a cool place away from sunlight. To turn it into an Italian seasoning, mix two tablespoons with ⅔cup of olive oil, ¼ cup of vinegar and two tablespoons of water.
Shake vigorously, and then shake immediately before use.

Dry Tomato Dressing

- 1 C. Dried tomatoes
- 1 teaspoon dried basil
- 1 teaspoon garlic powder
- ½ c. water
- 3 tablespoons of balsamic vinegar
- 2 C. Olive oil

Add all the ingredients except the oil to a blender and mix until smooth. Slowly add the olive oil while mixing. Serve fresh!

NOTE: Due to the low vinegar content, this dressing should not be kept in the refrigerator for more than seven days.

Caramelized onions are the secret of many tasty preparations: incredible stews, French onion soup and delicious sour cream sauce. To get that rich flavor, you need to cook the onions for quite some time, convince them to a deep dark brown color and mix them before they turn black. Take your time and enjoy. Once the onions are dry, you can grind them into a coarse powder that you can put in the woods with a bite of dry broth for a cup of delicious soup on the go. Or dip them in a little water and fold them in minced meat for a particularly tasty meatloaf.

MAKES 1¼ CUPS [175 G]
  - 1 tbsp butter
  - 1 tablespoon of olive oil or rapeseed oil
  - 2 pound onions [910 g], peeled, cut and thinly sliced
  - 4 sprigs of fresh thyme
  - 1 teaspoon of fine sea salt
  - 1/4 teaspoon freshly ground black pepper
  - 1 cup [240 ml] of dry sherry or white wine such as Riesling

1. In a large heavy-bottomed pan over medium heat, heat the butter and olive oil. Add onions and sprigs of thyme and mix well. Cook without discomfort until the onions start to brown. Stir with a wooden spoon, scraping all the sticky brown pieces from the bottom of the pan. Turn the heat to medium-low, add salt and pepper and continue to cook, stirring and scraping when a brown coating builds up in the pan. If the brown layer turns black quickly, reduce the heat.
After about 30 minutes of cooking, add 1/2 cup [120 ml] of sherry and scrape the bottom of the pan well. After another 10 minutes, add the remaining 1/2 cup [120 ml] of sherry and scrape again. Continue to cook until the onions are very soft and until the chestnut is uniform. (If the onions always become too dark, add a little water and scratch the pan again.) Leave to cool and remove the thyme sprigs.

2. Cover the dryer trays with non-stick leather fruit sheets.

3. Distribute the onion mixture on the prepared trays and press down to obtain as thin a layer as possible. Dry at 135 ° F [57 ° C] for 14-18 hours, until the onions

are crunchy. Some thicker areas may be more flexible, but the edges must be broken. Let it cool completely.

4. Peel the layer of dried onion from the non-stick sheet and cut it into smaller pieces. If desired, grind a coarse powder in a meat grinder or food processor, working in batches. It's okay to leave a few larger pieces of onion; they will be very soft when rehydrated.

5. Store in an airtight container, preferably with a pack of silica gel to prolong freshness, in a dark place at room temperature for up to 3 months or in the freezer for up to 1 year.

I won't lie; I was trying to make wasabi peas. But with domestic dehydrators, unlike industrial freeze dryers, a crisis is not always guaranteed. Sometimes a leathery consistency is obtained, such as dried or dried apricots, and sometimes thick food bites are obtained which are only good to rehydrate. This is what happened to my wasabi peas.

But I still liked the idea of a crunchy green snack with an excellent umami flavor, so I prepared this recipe with sliced green beans mixed with ginger, garlic and soy marinade. I think you will find that they go with a crunchy beer almost as good as wasabi peas.

Keep in mind that, as with many crispy dehydrating delicacies, it is best to consume these beans shortly after drying; soon they begin to lose the contraction.

MAKES 4 TO 6 SNACK PORTIONS
- 455 g of fresh green beans, without stem, without wire, if necessary, and cut diagonally in 1/4 mm [6 mm] shavings
- 2 tablespoons of soy sauce
- 1 clove of garlic, peeled and minced
- 1 teaspoon grated peeled fresh ginger
- 1/2 teaspoon of sesame oil

1. Cover the dehydrating trays with non-stick netting sheets lightly coated with cooking oil.

2. Bring a pan of salted water to a boil over medium-high heat. Add the green beans and cook until tender and crispy, about 2 minutes. Filter and then run cold water over the beans for about 1 minute to stop the cooking process.

3. In a medium non-reactive bowl, mix soy sauce, garlic, ginger and sesame oil. Add the drained beans and stir. Leave to marinate, stirring once or twice, for 15 minutes. Drain the green beans, reserving the dressing to serve as a dressing for rice or noodles.

4. Place the green beans on the prepared trays. Dry at 135 ° F [57 ° C] for 4-6 hours, until the beans are very dry and crunchy. Let it cool completely.

5. Store in an airtight container, preferably with a pack of silica gel to prolong freshness, in a dark place at room temperature for up to 2 weeks.

I often like to triple the sesame flavor, as with these French fries, which use cabbage for curly and chapped edges. In the marinade, I combine tahini, the sesame paste that you can have when you play a game of hummus, with the sauteed base sesame oil. Then I add a handful of toasted sesame seeds for an extra consistency.

MAKES 4 TO 6 SNACK PORTIONS
- 1 tablespoon of Tahini
- 1/4 teaspoon sesame oil
- 1 tablespoon of olive oil
- 1/2 teaspoon of fine sea salt
- 1 tablespoon of fresh lemon juice
- 1 clove of garlic, peeled and minced
- 1 head of cabbage, washed, destemmed and torn into pieces of 2 to 3 inches [5 to 7.5 cm]
- 1 tablespoon of toasted sesame seeds

1. Cover the dehydrating trays with non-stick netting sheets lightly coated with cooking oil.

2. In a small bowl, mix the tahin, sesame oil, olive oil, salt, lemon juice and garlic together.

3. Put the cabbage in a large bowl. Pour the tahini dressing on the sheets and massage the cabbage sheets well. Mix with the sesame seeds.

4. Place the cabbage pieces on the prepared trays. Dry at 135 ° F [57 ° C] for 5-7 hours, until all parts of the cabbage are dry. Let it cool completely.

5. Store in an airtight container, preferably with a silica gel pack to prolong freshness, in a dark place at room temperature for up to 3 days.

This recipe can win the prize for the prettiest snack bar: many airy flounces in dark burgundy, saffron orange and ivory white. I have found that a strong and sharp potato peeler is a great tool for preparing dehydration projects, and here I use mine to cut solid root vegetables into thin strips. Bleaching the vegetables before drying helps to unify their textures and also rushes during drying. Like many of the crunchy vegetable snacks in this chapter, it is best to eat them shortly after drying when they are crunchier. However, slightly less crunchy ribbons can be mixed in soups to add flavor and nutrition.

MAKES 4 TO 6 SNACK PORTIONS
- 2 medium parsnips, peeled
- 2 medium carrots, peeled
- 1 small beetroot, peeled
- 1 tablespoon of olive oil
- 1/2 teaspoon curry powder
- 3/4 teaspoon of sea salt

1. Cover the dehydrating trays with non-stick netting sheets lightly coated with cooking oil.

2. Bring a large pot of salted water to a boil over medium-high heat. Fill a large bowl with ice water.

3. While the water is warming up, use a sharp potato peeler to tie the parsnips, leaving the wood center behind. Repeat the process to create carrot strips and book separately. Repeat the process to create beetroot ribbons.

4. Put the parsnip strips in boiling water and cook for 30 seconds. Using a slotted spoon or a spider, remove the tapes and place them directly in the ice water. After the parsnip strips have cooled, remove them from the water and place them on a clean tea towel to dry. Repeat with the carrot strips, then with the beet strips, keeping the vegetables separate.

5. In a small pan over medium heat, add olive oil and curry and mix to mix. When the oil becomes fragrant, after about 11/2 minutes, remove it from the heat.

6. In a medium bowl, mix the parsnip strips with about a third of the curry oil and about 1/4 teaspoon of salt and mix well. Repeat with the carrot ribbons and then with the beetroot ribbons.

7. Place the vegetable ribbons on the prepared trays. Dry at 135 ° F [57 ° C], until it is tangled and completely crisp. Parsnips should be made in 6-8 hours, and carrots and beets can take 8 to 10 hours. Let it cool completely.

8. Peel the vegetable strips from the non-stick sheets and mix them on the work surface.

9. Store in an airtight container, preferably with a silica gel pack to prolong freshness, in a dark place at room temperature for up to 1 week.

This recipe makes dried tomatoes more elegant than I have ever seen. The peel of the cherry tomatoes is peeled and the pulp is removed, leaving only the "fillets" of tomato meat. Drying the tomato fillets for a few hours in a relatively hot dehydrator intensely concentrates the flavor of the tomato without making it too chewy or chewy.

Once you have these perfect red tomato petals, what are you doing with them? Roll them with a pinch of goat cheese as an appetizer; cut and mix with angel hair pasta, olive oil and basil for an intense version of a fresh pasta sauce; or decorate with them an elegant fish dish.

They are special and well worth it.

MAKES APPROXIMATELY 4 OZ [115 G]
-   16 plum tomatoes
-   1 teaspoon of fine sea salt
-   2 tablespoons of olive oil and more if necessary
-   11/2 teaspoons of fresh thyme sheets

1. Cover the dryer trays with non-stick leather fruit sheets.

2. Bring a large pot of water to a gentle boil over medium-high heat. Fill a large bowl with ice water.

3. Mark an X through the skin on the pointed end of each tomato. When the water boils, put about four tomatoes in the pot. After about 45 seconds, use a spoon or a perforated spider to remove the tomatoes and place them directly in the ice water. Peel the blanched tomatoes. Bring the water to a boil again and repeat the process with the remaining tomatoes.

4. When peeled, cut each tomato into quarters. Remove and discard the seeds and pulp from each quarter. Put the fleshy tomato petals in a large bowl and season with salt. Gently mix with olive oil and thyme.

5. Place the tomato petals on the prepared trays. Dry at 160 ° F [71 ° C] for 2-4 hours, until the tomatoes have a somewhat opaque surface and have halved. Let it cool completely.

6. Store in an airtight container in the refrigerator for up to 3 days or cover completely with olive oil and keep in the refrigerator for up to 1 month.

Meat Balls with Sauerkraut

Yield: 5 generous portions
- 3 cups of cooked, dehydrated meat
- 3 ¼ cups of water
- 2 tablespoons of dehydrated onion
- 2 cups of cold-cooked cereals
- 1 teaspoon salt
- ¼ teaspoon pepper
- ½ teaspoon celery salt
- 1 egg or 2 yolks, not beaten
- 3 and a half cups of sauerkraut and juice
- ⅓ cup of brown sugar, very compact
- 2 spoons of vinegar

1. Immerse the meat in 3 cups of water until it is reconstituted. Drain the water from the reconstituted meat; grind the meat in the meat grinder—Reserve ¼ cup of liquid for later use. Dip the onion in ¼ cup of water until it reconstitutes, then drain.

2. Combine ground beef, cereals, onion, salt, pepper, celery salt and eggs. Mix well, form balls and brown slowly on all sides in a dripping pan.

3. Pour the sauerkraut and juice over the meat and mix, then add the brown sugar, the reserved liquid and the vinegar.

4. Cover and simmer for about 20 minutes, or until the meatballs are finished, and the onion and egg mixture is cooked.

Old Fashion Hash

Yield: 3-4 portions
- 1 ½ cups of pieces of cooked, dehydrated meat
- 2 cups of dehydrated potatoes
- ¼ cup of dehydrated onion
- 3 ¾ cups of water
- 1 ¼ teaspoon salt
- ⅛ teaspoon pepper
- 2 and a half tablespoons of butter or margarine

1. Immerse the meat in 1 ½ cups of water until reconstitution, then drain. Dip the onion in half a glass of water until it reconstitutes. Empty and reserve the liquid. Immerse the potatoes in 2 cups of water until reconstitution, then cover the potatoes and cook over medium heat until they are tender. Drain the water, reserving it for later, and cool the potatoes. When it is cold, cut it into ¼ inch cubes.

2. Put the beef, chopped potatoes, onion, salt and pepper in a bowl. Stir lightly with a fork until well mixed.

3. Melt the butter or margarine in a pan and add 1 ¼ cups of the reserved liquid. Heat to a boil, then add the meat mixture. Stir gently, then cover and cook over medium heat until the meat is browned on one side, about 15 minutes. Rotate carefully with a spatula and, if necessary, add a little more butter or margarine. Cover and brown the mixture, but do not cook hashish too dry. The total cooking time is between 20 and 25 minutes.

4. Serve with chili sauce.

Yield: 4-6 portions
- 2 cups of pieces of cooked, dehydrated meat
- ¼ cup of dehydrated onion
- 2 ½ cups of water
- 4 tablespoons of butter or margarine
- ½ cup of sauce or 1 cube of beef broth mixed with ½ cup of hot water
- 1 teaspoon prepared horseradish
- ¼ teaspoon salt
- 2 cups of medium white sauce
- Half a kilo of mushrooms, clean and chopped
- ¼ cup of finely chopped parsley or 2 tablespoons of dehydrated parsley
- 1 batch of standard biscuit dough with 2 cups of flour

1. Immerse the meat in 2 cups of water until it is reconstituted, then grind the drained meat in an oil mill. Dip the onion in ½ cup of water until it reconstitutes, then drain.

2. Dissolve 2 tablespoons of butter or margarine in a pan and add the drained onions. Fry the onions until slightly transparent, about 5 minutes. Add ground beef, ½ cup sauce or reconstituted broth, horseradish and ¼ cup medium white sauce to the onions. Let it cool down.

3. Roll the cookie dough into a 9 × 12-inch rectangle. Distribute with the meat mixture, then roll up like the jelly roll. Seal the edges and cut into 8 cross slices. Place on a greased baking sheet cut face down.

4. Bake at 425 ° F for 25-30 minutes. Cover the pinwheels for the first 15 minutes with parchment paper to prevent them from drying out.

5. Melt the remaining butter or margarine in a saucepan, then add and brown the mushrooms. When the mushrooms are sautéed, add the salt and the remaining white sauce. Heat the mixture until it boils, then add the parsley. Serve hot on oven grinders.

Meat or Chicken Turnover

Yield: 5 portions
- 1 cup of cooked, dehydrated meat or pieces of chicken
- 1 ¼ cups of water
- ½ teaspoon of dehydrated onion
- 1 tablespoon of dehydrated celery
- 2 spoons of butter
- 2 tablespoons of flour
- 1 cube of beef or chicken broth
- 1 batch of standard biscuit dough with 2 cups of flour

1. Immerse the beef or chicken in 1 cup of water until reconstitution; drain, reserving ⅔ cup of liquid. Dip the onion and celery in ¼ cup of water until reconstituted, then drain. Boil the reserved liquid and mix in a cube of broth.

2. Melt the butter in a saucepan and brown the drained meat. Stir the flour until smooth, then gradually add the reserved liquid. Stir constantly over medium heat until smooth and dense. Add the drained onion and celery, then add salt and pepper to taste. Stir to mix and cool slightly.

3. Prepare the recipe for baking the cookie dough according to the instructions. Turn off on a floured board and roll or tap into a rectangle 6 × 15 inches ⅛inches thick. Cut into 5 pieces of 3 × 6 inches. Put ⅕of the cooked meat mixture in the middle of each piece of pasta. Moisten the edges and fold the other half over the meat. Press the edges together with the fork teeth to seal. Cut the design above the turnovers for the steam outlets.

4. Bake on a baking sheet greased at 425 ° F for 15-20 minutes or until the crust turns golden brown. Serve immediately with mushrooms, peas or other vegetables with cream.

Across Seattle, gourmets and cheerful club jumpers struggle to resist the sweet teriyaki soy call, sold in the city's corner stores. It may be the most popular cheap food in my city (although the Vietnamese sandwiches, *banh mi*, give it solid competition). The combination of soy sauce and ginger is a natural complement as an irregular marinade.

In this recipe, I softened the sugar a little so that the jerky dries well and isn't too sticky.

MAKES ABOUT 1 LB [455 G]
- 910 g round beef (London roast), fat free
- A piece of 4 inches [10 cm] ginger cut into 12 mm [1/2 inch] discs
- 3 cloves of garlic, peeled and minced
- 1 bunch of green onions, only green tops
- 1 dried chili pepper, like Japanese
- 1 cup [240 ml] of mirin (Japanese rice wine) or sherry
- 3/4 cup soy sauce [180 ml]
- 4 teaspoons of kosher salt
- 1/4 teaspoon freshly ground black pepper
- 2 tablespoons of brown sugar

1. Put the meat in the freezer for about 1 hour, until it becomes solid but not rigid. This will make it easier to cut the meat into thin slices. Cut the meat diagonally across the grain into 1/8 inch [3 mm] slices.

2. In a saucepan over medium-high heat, combine ginger, garlic, green onions, chilli pepper, mirin, soy sauce, salt, pepper and brown sugar and bring to a boil. Lower the heat, stir and simmer for 2 minutes.
Remove from the heat and allow to cool completely. Strain the marinade, pour over the sliced meat and mix to coat. Cover and refrigerate overnight.

3. Cover the trays of the dryer with non-stick mesh sheets lightly coated with cooking oil.

4. Distribute the slices of meat on the prepared trays. Dry at a temperature between 160 ° and 165 ° F [71 ° to 74 ° C] for 3-5 hours, until it darkens uniformly, completely opaque and rigid but still slightly flexible. (A cold slice of jerky should break when folded but should not break.)

Turn the strips over once and rotate the trays once or twice while drying. Remove from the dehydrator and wrap the uneven slices in paper towels to absorb excess fat. Let it cool completely.

5. Store in an airtight container, preferably with a pack of silica gel to prolong freshness, in a dark place at room temperature for 1 week, in the refrigerator for 2 weeks or in the freezer for 6 months.

I love being the one who carves a roast meat on Sunday, largely because it gives me a bite of access to the tasty crispy outer edges. I think of this basic beef jerky recipe as a way to recreate that chewy, slightly spicy and delicious part of the roast. Good old-fashioned garlic powder, salt, pepper and a little smoked paprika are a wonderful combination of toppings that provide some appetite for Sunday roast even when walking on a bumpy path or treating yourself to an afternoon snack.

- About $1^1/_4$ LB [570 G]
- 1.2 kg [21/2 lb] round beef, fat free
- $3^3/_4$ teaspoon kosher salt
- 1/2 teaspoon freshly ground black pepper
- 1 teaspoon garlic powder base
- 1/2 teaspoon smoked paprika or 1 teaspoon paprika

1. Put the meat in the freezer for about 1 hour, until it becomes solid but not rigid. This will make it easier to cut the meat into thin slices. Cut the meat diagonally across the grain into 1/8 inch [3 mm] slices.

2. in a large bowl, mix salt, pepper, powdered garlic and paprika. Mix the slices of meat with the salt mixture, making sure to separate the slices so as to distribute the seasoning evenly. Cover and refrigerate overnight.

3. Cover the trays of the dryer with non-stick mesh sheets lightly coated with cooking oil.

4. Distribute the slices of meat on the prepared trays. Dry at a temperature between 160 ° and 165 ° F [71 ° to 74 ° C] for 3-5 hours, until it darkens uniformly, completely opaque and rigid but still slightly flexible. (A cold slice of jerky should break when folded but should not break.) Turn the strips over once and rotate the trays once or twice while drying. Remove from the dehydrator and wrap the uneven slices in paper towels to absorb excess fat. Let it cool completely.

5. Store in an airtight container, preferably with a pack of silica gel to prolong freshness, in a dark place at room temperature for 1 week, in the refrigerator for 2 weeks or in the freezer for 6 months.

Bite into this shot, and it's easy to imagine that you're relaxing in a camp in the middle of a scrub-stained spot and the campfire is sending out puffs of musky smoke. Since you don't generally smoke in spurts while it is being created, I often like to add a little smoked aroma to my marinades by adding smoked condiments. Chipotle peppers are actually smoked, cheap, easy to find jalapeños and pack a world of flavors in a small can. It is so tasty, in fact, that you won't even use a whole can of peppers for a series of rips. Try crushing the chipotle left in a mayonnaise blender to distribute a spicy sandwich.

ABOUT $1^{1}/_{4}$ LB [570 G]
- 1.2 kg [$2^{1}/_{2}$ lbs] round beef, fat free
- 1/4 cup chopped chipotle chile [60 g] in adobo sauce
- 1 tablespoon of olive oil
- 1 clove of garlic, peeled and minced
- $3^{3}/_{4}$ teaspoon kosher salt

1. Put the meat in the freezer for about 1 hour until it is firm but not stiff. This will make it easier to cut the meat into thin slices. Cut the meat diagonally across the grain into 1/8 inch [3 mm] slices.

2. In a large bowl, mix the chilli pepper, olive oil, garlic and salt. Mix the slices of meat in the chipotle mix, making sure to separate the slices so as to distribute the seasoning evenly. Cover and refrigerate overnight or up to 24 hours.

3. Cover the trays of the dryer with non-stick mesh sheets lightly coated with cooking oil.

4. Distribute the slices of meat on the prepared trays. Dry at a temperature between 160 ° and 165 ° F [71 ° to 74 ° C] for 3-5 hours, until it darkens uniformly, completely opaque and rigid but still slightly flexible. (A cold slice of jerky should break when folded but should not break.) Turn the strips over once and rotate the trays once or twice while drying. Remove from the dehydrator and wrap the uneven slices in paper towels to absorb excess fat. Let it cool completely.

5. Store in an airtight container, preferably with a pack of silica gel to prolong freshness, in a dark place at room temperature for 1 week, in the refrigerator for 2 weeks or in the freezer for 6 months.

Buffalo meat is naturally quite lean and therefore excellent for squabble. I also love using these classic spiced elk hunter spices, which is more difficult to find (unless you are a hunter). If you use wild play, be especially careful. Use only game meat that has been frozen at -15 ° C for at least 4 days before continuing with this recipe. And if you grind the meat yourself, follow all the signs for North African Spiced Beef Jerky (page 118). The instructions here are for prepared buffalo meat because it is what is most commonly found on the meat counter for these special meats. Ground meat jerks like this are easier to model with a jerky gun (see page 16). If you don't have a trigger gun, you can approximate the strips by using a pastry bag with a wide, flat tip or by pressing the meat into 5 x 10 cm strips with the back of a spoon.

MAKES ABOUT 1 LB [455 G]
- 6 juniper berries
- $3^1/_2$ teaspoons of kosher salt
- 1/4 teaspoon freshly ground black pepper
- 1/4 teaspoon ground cloves
- 910 g of ground buffalo, elk or lean beef
- 2 bay leaves
- 1 teaspoon minced garlic
- 1 tablespoon of olive oil
- 1/4 cup [60 ml] of gin

1. The evening before drying the meat, use a meat grinder or mortar to grind or grind the juniper berries and 1/2 teaspoon salt in a coarse powder. In a small bowl, mix the juniper powder together with the remaining 3 teaspoons of salt, pepper and cloves.

2. In a medium bowl, mix minced meat, bay sheets, garlic, olive oil and gin together with the spice mixture. Cover and refrigerate overnight.

3. Cover the trays of the dryer with non-stick mesh sheets lightly coated with cooking oil.

4. Remove the bay sheets from the meat mixture and throw them away. Stir the meat mixture again.

5. Place the meat mixture in strips of 5 x 10 cm, approximately 3 mm thick, on the prepared trays. It is useful to use a butter knife to carefully cut the end of each strip of meat.
Dry at a temperature between 160 ° and 165 ° F [71 ° to 74 ° C] for 4 to 6 hours, drying occasionally with paper towels, until it dries to the touch, not pink in the center and still a little flexible. Remove from the dehydrator and dry again with paper towels. Let it cool completely.

6. Store in an airtight container, preferably with a pack of silica gel to prolong freshness, in a dark place at room temperature for up to 3 days, in the refrigerator for up to 1 week or in the freezer for up to 6 months.

If there is a combination of condiments that I hope to appreciate for the rest of my life, it is the hot spices that are used throughout North Africa: spicy cumin, lemon coriander, sweet aniseed fennel seeds and a warm touch spicy pepper. Here, I bite the food processor's lean lamb leg to make a chewy tear, almost like sausage. It is an unexpectedly complex taste to be jerky. To create beef jerky strips, it is easier to use a jerky gun, but see the main notes of Buffalo Jerky with Gin Botanicals for alternatives.

MAKES ABOUT 1 LB [455 G]
- 910 g fat-free rack of lamb, cut into small pieces
- 1 tablespoon of cumin seeds
- 1 teaspoon coriander seeds
- 1 teaspoon of chili flakes
- 1/2 teaspoon fennel seeds
- 1/4 teaspoon smoked paprika
- 1/4 teaspoon ground cinnamon
- 4 teaspoons of kosher salt
- 2 cloves of garlic, peeled and minced
- 1 tablespoon of olive oil

1. Put the lamb in the freezer for about 1 hour to firm it up.

2. In a dry pan over medium heat, combine the cumin seeds, coriander seeds, red pepper flakes and fennel seeds. Cook until the cumin seeds have slightly darkened and toasted, 30 to 60 seconds. Let it cool completely.

3. In a spice grinder or mortar and pestle, pulverize the roasted spices in a fine powder. In a small bowl, mix with the smoked paprika, cinnamon and salt.

4. Grind the lamb using the fine blade of a meat grinder or pressing it into a food processor (works in batches if you are using a food processor). In a medium bowl, mix the ground lamb with the mixture of spices, garlic and olive oil. Cover and refrigerate overnight.

5. Cover the dehydrator trays with non-stick mesh sheets lightly coated with cooking oil.

6. Place the meat mixture in strips of 5 by 10 cm of thickness of about 3 mm on the prepared trays. It is useful to use a butter knife to carefully cut the end of each strip of meat. Dry at a temperature between 160 ° and 165 ° F [71 ° to 74 ° C] for 4-6 hours, until dry to the touch, not pink in the center and still a little flexible. Turn the strips over once and rotate the trays once or twice while drying. Remove from the dryer and wrap the uneven strips in paper towels to absorb excess fat. Let it cool completely.

7. Store in an airtight container, preferably with a pack of silica gel to prolong freshness, in a dark place at room temperature for up to 3 days, in the refrigerator for 1 week or in the freezer for up to 6 months.

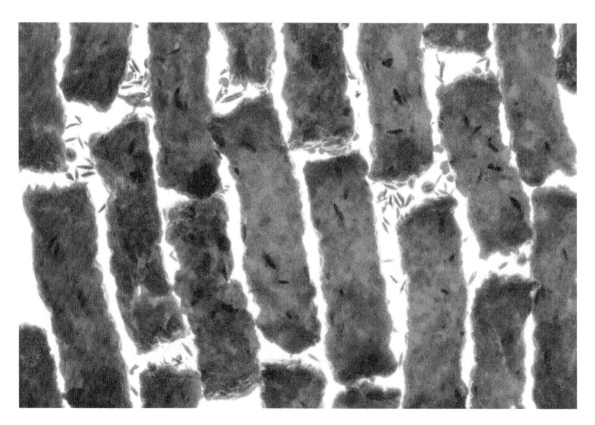

I haven't been to Malaysia, but I've been to Richmond, British Columbia, near Vancouver, where you can make almost any type of Asian snack you could wish for, including Malaysian pork, soy sweet, flavored with fish sauce and Grilled with care on special low heat steel grates.

I decided to try the delicious mix in my dehydrator myself. Do not use pre-packed minced pork from the local butcher; It usually contains a lot of fat and you will want the leanest meat possible, such as pork loin. It's easy to cut the food processor, or you can ask a trusted butcher to grind it finely. While I give instructions to dry like other balls, I also offer an alternative.

For some freshly grilled flavor, throw some almost finished shots under the grill for a minute or two until the sugar in the shots starts to caramelize.

To create beef jerky strips, it is easier to use a jerky gun, but see the main notes of Buffalo Jerky with Gin Botanicals for alternatives.

About 1¼ LB [570 G]
- 1.2 kg of pork loin, oily and silver skin cut and cut into 2.5 cm pieces
- 1/4 cup [60 ml] Shaoxing wine (Chinese rice wine) or dry white wine such as Riesling
- 60 ml of fish sauce
- 1/2 cup [100 g] of sugar
- 3 tablespoons of soy sauce
- 2 cloves of garlic, peeled and minced
- 1/2 teaspoon pepper flakes or to taste
- 1 tablespoon of kosher salt

1. In a food processor, combine pork, wine, fish sauce, sugar, soy sauce, garlic, chilli pepper and salt. (If you have a small machine, you may need to work in batches.) Clean at 5-second intervals, occasionally scraping the bowl until the meat is finely and evenly minced. Scrape the minced pork mixture in a medium bowl, cover and refrigerate overnight.

2. Cover the trays of the dryer with non-stick mesh sheets lightly coated with cooking oil. (If you are roasting or roasting the jerk, cover each tray with a sheet of non-stick leather for fruit.)

3. Place the meat mixture in strips of 5 x 10 cm of thickness of about 3 mm on the prepared trays. It is useful to use a butter knife to carefully cut the end of each strip of meat. Dry from 160 ° to 165 ° F [71 ° to 74 ° C] for 4 to 6 hours, drying occasionally with paper towels, until dry to the touch but still a little flexible. (If you're going to roast the jerk and have used fruit skin sheets on the trays, the bottom of the jerk will cook but won't dry - it will finish drying and turn brown in the oven.)

4. If desired, place a grill on the oven and preheat the grill. Remove the jerk from the dehydrator and place the jerk with the pale side facing up on the grill pan. Grill until the edges of the jerk are caramel colored. It may be necessary to work in batches. Let it cool completely.

5. Store in an airtight container, preferably with a pack of silica gel to prolong freshness, in a dark place at room temperature for up to 3 days, in the refrigerator for 1 week or in the freezer for up to 6 months.

This recipe was my attempt to make the soft dry pork product called pork tenderloin (also wool or bah-sang wool) popular in China and Taiwan, which is the dry pork that simulates the texture of cotton candy and is used. as a meaty condiment to give depth to any number of comfort foods, from rice porridge (congee) to tofu and stir-fried noodles; in fact, I called that magic paste powder. He could not duplicate the airy texture of the commercial product; instead, the pig is dried in crisp and short pieces. I found that I liked the pig in powder more often, and that's what I recommend you try. This recipe is basically dehydrated Hunan-style red pork. Feel free to taste some of the pork stew as you prepare it, drying the leftovers.

MAKES ABOUT 8 OZ [230 G]
- Pork shoulder cut [910 g] 2 lbs, cut into cubes
- 2 tablespoons of brown sugar
- 2 spoons of vegetable oil
- 4 garlic cloves, peeled
- Star anise 3
- 3 green onions, white and light green parts, cut and sliced
- 2 tablespoons of soy sauce
- 360 ml of low sodium or water chicken broth

1. Dry the pork cubes with a paper towel. In a large saucepan over medium heat, combine the brown sugar and vegetable oil, stirring until the sugar dissolves a little. Add the pork and brown, stirring occasionally, for 5-7 minutes.

2. Add garlic, star anise, green onions, soy sauce and broth to the pan. Bring to a boil, lower the heat to simmer and cover the pot. Remove the grayish foam from the surface of the liquid and cook the meat until a sample cube can be easily broken with two forks, about 1 hour and 45 minutes. Drain the pork, place it on a large plate and refrigerate until it is easy to handle. When cold, tear the pork with two forks, removing large pieces of fat.

3. Cover the trays of the dryer with non-stick mesh sheets lightly coated with cooking oil. Cover the bottom of the dehydrator with a sheet of non-stick mesh for easy cleaning.

4. Place the pork on the prepared trays. Dry from 74 ° to 77 ° C [165 ° to 170 ° F] for 8 to 10 hours, drying occasionally with paper towels, until it becomes crisp. When dry, place the dried pork on paper towels to dry more. Let it cool completely. You can keep the meat in pieces or, using a food processor (or a blender), grind the pork pieces into a coarse powder.

5. Store in an airtight container, preferably with a silica gel pack to prolong freshness, in a dark place for up to 1 week, in the refrigerator for up to 2 weeks or in the freezer for up to 6 months.

Turkey will become firmer than other meats in the dehydrator, so this jerk really earns his name.

You might be surprised by the richness of flavors imparted by the sage and garlic marinade used here. It is somewhat Italian in the southern United States, thanks to a sweet touch of molasses, which plays an interesting role. Although the meat is completely cooked in the highest position of the dehydrator, it tends to appear a little pale; molasses gives the meat an earthy sweetness and also an attractive irregular tone.

MAKES ABOUT 1 LB [455 G]
- 1 kg turkey breast
- 2 spoons of olive oil
- 3 garlic cloves, peeled and sliced
- 8 sage sheets
- 2 tbsp molasses
- 1/4 teaspoon freshly ground black pepper
- 21/2 teaspoons of kosher salt

1. Remove the skin from the turkey breast and put it in the freezer for 2 to 4 hours, until it becomes firm but not frozen. Cut the meat diagonally across the grain into 1/8 inch [3 mm] slices. Cut any large slice into 5 cm wide strips.

2. In a small saucepan over medium heat, heat the olive oil. Add garlic and sage and cook 1 or 2 minutes, until it is fragrant. Add the molasses and pepper, remove from the heat and allow to cool to room temperature.

3. In a large bowl, mix the turkey slices with the salt and molasses mixture, making sure all slices are evenly covered. Cover and refrigerate overnight.

4. Cover the trays of the dryer with non-stick mesh sheets lightly coated with cooking oil.

5. Place the turkey slices on the prepared trays. Dry at a temperature between 160 ° and 165 ° F [71 ° to 74 ° C] for 3-5 hours, drying occasionally with paper towels, until it is very dry to the touch but still slightly flexible. Let it cool completely.

6. Store in an airtight container, preferably with a pack of silica gel to prolong freshness, in a dark place at room temperature for up to 1 week, in the refrigerator for up to 2 weeks or in the freezer for up to 6 months.

Here in the Northwest Pacific, smoked and scmi-dried "salmon caramel" is a popular snack. You will find it in specialty food stores and small coastal shops. I love chewing sweet salmon in depth, but I don't like so much sweetness because it masks the taste of fresh salmon. This is my recipe, with maple syrup instead of brown sugar and a pinch of paprika to give it a smoked flavor without the hours of smoking. Look for sockeye or silver salmon (coho) for this recipe: they are less fat than real salmon or chinook, which are very expensive and work best for dry recipes.

MAKES ABOUT2/3 LB [320 G]
- 680 g of salmon or silver fillet
- 1/2 cup [120 ml] of soy sauce
- 60 ml of maple syrup
- 1/2 teaspoon freshly ground black pepper
- 1 teaspoon smoked paprika

1. Remove the pin bones from the salmon with tweezers or forceps. (To find the bones, slide your fingers along the edge of the fillet from the end of the head to the tail. The flexible pin bones are lined up in a row.) Cut all the other bones near the fish's belly area. Starting at the end of the fillet head, use a very sharp knife to cut the part fish into 1/4 inch [6 mm] slices. Put in a large bowl and refrigerate mixing the marinade.

2. In a small bowl, mix the soy sauce, maple syrup, pepper and paprika together. Pour the mixture over the salmon slices and mix gently to coat. Leave to marinate for 3 hours, then drain the fish thoroughly. If it does not dry immediately, place the drained salmon slices on a plate, cover and refrigerate for up to 12 hours.

3. Cover the trays of the dryer with non-stick mesh sheets lightly coated with cooking oil.
4. Place the salmon on the prepared trays. Dry at a temperature between 160 ° and 165 ° F [71 ° to 74 ° C] for 3-5 hours, drying occasionally with paper towels, until it is dry and tanned to the touch and chewy. Let it cool completely.

5. Store in an airtight container, preferably with a silica gel pack to prolong freshness, in the refrigerator for up to 2 weeks or in the freezer for up to 6 months.

Beef Broth

- 8 oz. Well marinated jerky beef, dry until it is very hard
- ½ c. Dried onion
- ½ c. Dry celery
- ¼ c. Dried pepper

This recipe works with any type of meat or fish. You will need an excellent food processor / blender. Break the jerk into pieces no more than an inch long and turn the powder into the food processor. Add the dried onion, celery and pepper, also reducing them to powder. Mix well and store in an airtight container away from sources of heat and light.

Pottage

- ½ c. Dry celery
- ½ c. Dried onion
- ¼ c. Dried carrot
- ¼ c. Dry red pepper
- ½ teaspoon salt
- 1 teaspoon garlic powder
- ¼ teaspoon black pepper

Put all the ingredients in a food processor and mix them into powder. Store in an airtight container in a dark place. Use 1 teaspoon and a half. broth per cup of water to prepare vegetable broth.

Mushroom Soup

- 1-½ c. Dried mushrooms
- ½ c. Dried onions
- 2 teaspoons of powdered beef broth
- 1 teaspoon salt
- ¼ c. Butter
- 4 c. water

Heat two cups of water until it boils in a saucepan, remove from the heat and add the mushrooms and dried onions. Let it sit for five minutes. Heat the butter in a pan over medium-low heat, remove the mushrooms and onion from the water with a perforated spoon and fry the mushrooms and onions in the butter, reserving the liquid in which they were immersed. Add two more cups of water, the powdered beef broth and the onions and mushrooms sautéed again in the saucepan. Put the saucepan back on the heat, bring to a boil, then reduce the heat and simmer, stirring occasionally, for fifteen minutes before serving.

Vegetable Noodles Soup

- 4 c. water
- 6 teaspoons of vegetable broth (from the recipe in this chapter) ½ c. Dried carrots
- ¼ c. Dried onions
- 1 garlic, small clove slices
- ½ c. Dried and diced potatoes
- 1 C. Fresh cabbage, thinly sliced
- 1 C. Dry egg pasta
- ½ teaspoon of oregano
- ½ teaspoon of basil
- 2 spoons of olive oil
- Salt and pepper to taste

Bring olive oil over medium heat in a pan and fry the cabbage and garlic until the cabbage is well wilted.
Combine all the ingredients (including cabbage and garlic from the previous step) in a medium skillet. Bring to a boil, stirring occasionally, then reduce the heat and simmer until the noodles are ready.

Beef Jerky Soup

- Jerky, broken beef or scissors cut into small 8 ounces. pieces
- 3 c. water
- 1 C. Red wine (does not cook wine; use the authentic one!)
- 2 teaspoons of vegetable broth (previous recipe)
- 1 teaspoon beef broth (previous recipe)

Simmer for two hours until the meat is tender. Then add the following:

- ½ c. Dehydrated potato cubes
- ½ c. Dehydrated carrots
- ¼ c. Dehydrated onion
- ¼ c. Dehydrated celery
- ½ teaspoon of garlic powder
- ½ teaspoon of oregano
- ½ teaspoon of dried basil
- ½ teaspoon dried thyme

Boil for another 30 minutes until everything is tender and melted. Serve hot.

Onion Soup

- 1 C. Dried onions
- ½ c. Beef broth powder (from a previous recipe)
- 2 tablespoons of onion powder
- 1 teaspoon black pepper

Combine the dry ingredients and store in an airtight container away from light. To prepare the onion soup, combine three tablespoons of the mixture with eight ounces of boiling water, let it stand covered for a few minutes, then enjoy.

Instant Vegetable Soup

- 1 teaspoon onion powder
- ½ teaspoon celery powder
- ½ teaspoon salt
- 1 dehydrated pepper, coarsely chopped spoons
- 1 dried carrot, coarsely chopped spoon
- 1 teaspoon of dehydrated tomato, coarsely chopped Store in an airtight package until use.

This recipe can be multiplied as many times as you want. Add a cup of boiling water to 3 tablespoons of instant vegetable soup. Stir and let stand five minutes before enjoying.

Trail Mixes

Tropical Mix

- 1 C. Dried coconut flakes
- ½ c. Dried pineapple
- ½ c. Dried mangoes or dried apricots

Cut all pieces no larger than ½ "in any size. Mix well. Store in an airtight container away from sunlight.

Fruit and Nuts Mix

- 1 C. Dried Apples
- ½ c. Dried Grapes (Raisins)
- ½ c. Dried prunes (prunes)
- ½ c. Dried bananas
- ½ c. Broken pecans
- ¼ c. pistachios

Cut apples and plums into pieces no larger than ½ "in any size. Break intact walnuts slightly. Pistachio shell if necessary. Mix well and store in an airtight container away from sunlight.

Sinfully Sweet Mix

- 1 C. Dried Apples
- ½ c. Dried Grapes (Raisins)
- ½ c. Bittersweet chocolate chips
- ½ c. almonds

Slightly break the almonds; cut the apples into pieces so that they are no larger than ½ "in any size. Mix well
Store in an airtight container in a cool, dry place away from sunlight.

Kid's Delight

- ½ c. Dried Apples
- ½ c. Dried bananas

- ½ c. Dried pineapple

Break, tear or cut pieces so that they are no larger than ½ "in any size. Mix well, then store in an airtight container away from sunlight.

High Protein Mix

- ½ c. Dried meat
- ¼ c. raisins
- ¼ c. Pumpkin seeds Pinch of dried, chopped or chopped seaweed

Dried meat is slightly salty, the raisins are sweet and the seaweed acts as a flavor enhancer, making it surprisingly tasty despite unusual ingredients. Cut the dried meat into pieces no larger than ½ "in any size. Add raisins and pumpkin seeds, then sprinkle with chopped or chopped dried seaweed. Mix well. Store in an airtight container away from sunlight.

Raw Kale Chips

- 2 Ibs. Swiss cabbage or Swiss chard
- ½ teaspoon of Celtic sea salt
- 1 lemon
- ½ teaspoon of garlic powder
- 2 spoons of olive oil
- 1 teaspoon of toasted sesame seed oil

Most people prefer black cabbage for this recipe, but I prefer Swiss chard because it better fits my digestion. Remove the large ribs from the cabbage and cut it into strips. (I think the scissors work better.) Put the strips in a large bowl. Quickly mix the oils, lemon juice, salt and garlic powder in a separate bowl, then pour the mixture onto the cabbage and mix it in the cabbage with your hands, so that it is completely covered.

Place the strips on the dehydrator trays and run the dehydrator at 145 degrees until the strips are crisp. Collect them carefully and store them in an airtight container. This will continue for two weeks.

Cinnamon Apples Crisps (I prefer Granny Smith, but any type will work)

- 1 teaspoon ground cinnamon
- ¼ c. Honey
- 1 lemon
- Non-stick spray oil

The secret to making dehydrated apples crisp and crunchy is to cut them into thin slices. I use what is called a "mandolin slicer" with a calibrated insert for ⅛". Peel and core the apples, then cut them into slices of ⅛". Put the apples in a large bowl. Spray a little non-stick cooking spray into a measuring cup and distribute it evenly, then add the honey to the measuring cup. Squeeze the juice of one lemon into the measuring cup.

Microwave the cup for ten seconds at a time until honey drips. Then add the cinnamon. Pour the mixture over the sliced apples and use your clean hands to cover them as evenly as possible. Lightly spray the trays of the dryer with non-stick cooking spray. (Otherwise, the honey will stick them to the trays like glue.) Place the covered apple slices on the dehydrator trays without overlapping and dehydrate at 150 degrees until crispy. Store in an airtight container away from sunlight. These will be kept for about a month.

Candied Fruit

- Fruit of your choice, sliced
- 1 C. sugar
- 1 C. Honey
- 1½ c. water
- Non-stick spray oil

Cut the fruit into pieces no larger than ½ ". Cut the berries, grapes and similar fruits in half.

Combine sugar, honey and water in a heavy saucepan and heat over medium heat until the temperature reaches 235 degrees on a caramel thermometer. Keep the temperature as close to 235 degrees as possible throughout the process.

Add ½ c. of fruit in syrup and let it boil until it is transparent at the edges, which will take between 10 and 20 minutes, depending on the fruit.

Use a perforated spoon to remove the fruit and distribute it on a dehydrator tray that has been sprayed with non-stick cooking spray.

Add the next batch of fruit to the syrup and repeat the process until all the fruit is in the dehydrator trays. Dehydrate at 135 degrees until it becomes chewy and a fruit torn in half and squeezed shows no humidity. It will be stored indefinitely in an airtight container.

Variation: add 1 tsp. Ground cinnamon, ½ tsp. Ground cloves and half a teaspoon. Jamaican pepper with syrup.

- 6 bananas, only ripe but not overripe
- ¼ c. Honey
- ½ lemons
- ½ teaspoon ground cinnamon
- Non-stick spray oil

As with the last recipe, the secret of crunchy bananas is to cut them into thin slices, no more than ⅛ "thick. If you cut them more often, they will be like stones and will break rather than break. Bananas are too delicate for a mandolin slicer, so I do it with the naked eye. If you are unfamiliar with measurements like this, look at a ruler to see how thick it is.

Cut the bananas into thin slices and put them in a medium bowl.
Lightly spray the inside of a measuring spoon with a non-stick cooking spray, then add the honey to the cup. Also squeeze half a lemon into the cup. Heat the measuring spoon in the microwave for 10 seconds at a time until honey drips, then add the cinnamon.

Pour the mixture over the bananas, then use your clean hands to make sure the banana slices are completely covered. Then lightly spray the dehydrator trays with non-stick cooking spray and place the banana slices on the trays without overlapping them. Dehydrate at 135 degrees until crispy. Store in an airtight container for up to two weeks.

- Summer squash (and / or zucchini)
- Celtic sea salt
- Freshly ground black pepper
- Melted Coconut Oil

If you've ever grown summer squash and planted too many plants, you know what I mean by "Summer Squash Surprise!"

The performances are so impressive that it is difficult to know what to do with everything! Well, here's an idea: turn your excess into crunchy potato chips! An advantage is that a friend of mine wants a chip that can be used with sauces and is also a friend of the paleo diet.

The quantity of each ingredient depends on the quantity of pumpkin (or zucchini) you have and your taste preferences. As with the other recipes in this section, the key is to thinly slice the pumpkin (or zucchini). Use a mandolin slicer to slice the pumpkin into even ⅛ "slices. Put the slices in a large bowl, pour some melted coconut oil over them and use your clean hands to lightly and evenly coat the pumpkin slices. Then add finely ground sea salt and freshly ground black pepper, using your clean hands again to distribute the salt and pepper completely.

Place the slices on the dehydrating trays and dehydrate at 135 degrees until crispy. Coconut oil is stable, so you can store them in an airtight container at room temperature for up to a month.

- Green beans
- Celtic sea salt
- Melted coconut oil

Green beans are an excellent crunchy snack. Steam blanches them for five minutes, soak them in ice water, and then pour them on some clean, soft towels to remove all the water. Place in a large bowl and use clean hands to distribute the coconut oil lightly and evenly among the beans.

Then add fine sea salt and distribute.

Place the beans on dehydrating trays and dehydrate at 135 degrees until they become crispy. These will be kept in an airtight container for up to one month.

Conclusion

You'll embark on an exciting journey with food dehydration, where you'll learn how to make healthy snacks and meals that inspire those around you. And since they're made with dehydrated ingredients, they're going to be easier and simpler to produce and safer. Follow the instructions in this book, and see the incredible benefits of dehydrated food. There will be no stopping you after that.

Printed in Great Britain
by Amazon